Analysing
Competence

The Kogan Page Practical Trainer Series

Series Editor: Roger Buckley

'*Excellent and challenging*' The Learning World, BBC World Service
'*Jargon-free and straightforward . . . sound advice*' Personnel Management
'*Clear, informative, very practically oriented*' The Training Officer

Analysing Competence

Tools and Techniques for Analysing Jobs, Roles and Functions

SHIRLEY FLETCHER

KOGAN PAGE

London • Stirling (USA)

First published in 1997

Kogan Page Limited
120 Pentonville Road
London N1 9JN ·
and ·
22883 Quicksilver Drive
Stirling, VA 20166, USA

British Library Cataloguing in Publication Data

A CIP record for this book is available from the British Library.

ISBN 0 7494 2195 9

Typeset by Key Composition, Northampton, Northamptonshire
Printed and bound in Great Britain by Biddles Ltd, Guildford and King's Lynn

Contents

List of Tables and Figures

Introduction

This book is about the relationships between the structure of work, the expectations of work and human performance. It is also about completing an analysis of these relationships, which provides the basis for a valuable and accepted vehicle for improving business performance.

Consultants, both internal and external, are employed to complete an analysis of 'competence' or to define competences/ies for various groups of staff. This often involves considerable research and the production of a plethora of lists, reports and analysis results. It may result in a competence framework or a task/role/job analysis which is well received by the project manager and the Human Resources Department. However, at the 'sharp end' the end-users often file this away and it is often forgotten.

The actual quality of the analysis work would not necessarily be in question in this type of scenario. The approach used and the expertise applied may be superb. The problem is more likely to be related to the lack of understanding of the *real need* for the analysis. Similarly, failure to consider the *actual and potential uses of the analysis results* can lead to this unsatisfactory outcome.

As with all effective research, the problem must first be clearly defined in order for an appropriate solution to be prepared. In many cases, consultants have a preferred solution which they try to apply to any given problem – an approach doomed to failure.

This book helps you to think innovatively to create a tailored solution for specific performance problems. It provides a toolkit for you to use and – as with any toolkit – you need to combine different tools to meet different needs. The phrase 'using a sledgehammer to crack a nut' often springs to mind in the context of a competence analysis. I hope that you will use this book in a more imaginative way, swopping your hammer for a more appropriate and effective tool, and even modifying the tool when needed. You will certainly be encouraged to combine tools to produce *real results*.

1

Competence: A Worldwide Concept

The increasing interest in competence and competence frameworks is demonstrated by the wide range of articles and publications that are devoted solely to this subject. Each of these may address the term 'competence' from a different perspective.

The references and further reading section in this book will give you an idea of how confusing this topic can be if you are not well prepared for the task in hand. Many organisations around the world have competences or competencies of one type or another. You must therefore be very clear about the basis for your analysis, which could be demands for competences to meet the needs of international executives, divisional managers, or specific roles, jobs or functions across an organisation.

You must be clear about the intended *users and uses* of the competences you are analysing and developing. You must also make a clear distinction between *competences and competencies* – both from your own and the generally accepted viewpoints (this issue is picked up later in this chapter).

Careful consideration of all these key points will enable you to plan your analysis and development to take account of all influencing factors, whether these be job or role related, functional or cross-functional, cultural, behavioural or multinational.

This chapter helps you to begin with the definition of your analysis and development project.

First Steps

I stated earlier that the best place to start any competence analysis is with a definition of the problem. In many cases, the first problem to define is a common understanding of the term 'competence'.

> *Without clarification of basic concepts and terminology your analysis will be a costly and time-wasting process.*

There are a few questions to be addressed *before* you plan your tools and techniques. Time spent on this activity is well invested.

It is surprising how often work on competence analysis is undertaken without clear goals and objectives. Consider the project plan shown in Table 1.1.

Table 1.1 *Example of project plan*

Project title	Competence development
Aim	To define competences for supervisors
Objectives	To produce a comprehensive list of competences relating to supervisors' roles To identify critical skills of supervisors To identify critical tasks of supervisors
Timescale	Six months
Methods	Critical incident analysis
Resources	Two part-time HR officers to conduct research and analysis, working 50% contracted time
Outcome	Competences defined for all supervisors
Evaluation	Results of consultation with supervisors on relevance and clarity of competences

What is wrong with this plan? Let's consider some aspects in more detail – see Table 1.2.

Table 1.2 *Review of the project plan in Table 1.1*

Aim and Outcome	This project results in competences defined for all supervisors. For what purpose? How are these competences to be used? Why are they being developed?
Objectives	If all objectives are achieved, what will we have? Basically, we have *lists* of skills, tasks, competences. Why do we want these?
Methods	Why critical incident analysis? What will this technique give us in terms of information about the supervisors' role? About the expectations of supervisors? About competence? How will the information obtained from use of this technique be analysed to produce competences?
General	What will the competences look like? What do we mean by 'competences'? Will the competences reflect *current or future* performance requirements? Are we talking about a supervisor's *job*, a supervisor's *role* or a supervisory *function*? Does the potential difference in terminology really make a difference?
Evaluation	If the supervisors are happy with the outcome – what next? Will the supervisors have any concerns about why the competences are being defined for them? Are we aiming to evaluate the method used to define the competences, or the competences themselves, or something else?

There are many more questions we could ask. This example – a real, if anonymous one – is typical of those produced in organisations of all sizes, and of those competence projects which ultimately die a quiet (or even painful) death.

There is often an unspoken assumption that 'developing competence/ies will improve performance'. This is an illogical and incorrect basis on which to proceed. Simply producing competences *will not* improve performance. I can think of many occasions where this development process has, through bad planning and poor communication, resulted in demotivated and cynical employees, thus leading to a reduction in overall performance.

Producing competences will provide – competences! How these competences are *used* is a key factor in improving business performance. Yet so many analysis and development projects ignore this point at the outset.

So Where Should You Start?

Let's suppose you have been asked to plan and implement a project to analyse and produce a competence framework for managers. What should your first question be?

What is the purpose of the competence framework?

You may receive answers such as:

- to clearly define the role of manager
- to identify what management skills we have
- to decide what we need in managers for the future.

You may even receive a few more!

The first answer is similar to our earlier example. If the only purpose is to define the role – why bother? Is there some further purpose? The second answer illustrates how people make assumptions about a common understanding of terms such as 'competence'. Is the individual who gave the answer assuming that 'competences' is another term for 'skills'? Is this the same assumption as everyone else is making? Is there also an assumption that analysing and defining competences for a management role is the same as identifying current individual or group skill levels? This is often an issue for confusion on two levels.

(a) Is the analysis about the role or about the people who hold the role?
(b) An analysis can identify what competences are needed for a role – to identify what skills/competences are currently available from role holders is a further step.

The third answer gives a little more information to work on. This individual is focused on the need to look forward and identify what is needed for managers of the future. This tells you that your analysis must be based on future plans. However, what you do not know is how this individual perceives 'competence'. Does he or she agree with the second respondent, ie, that competence = skills? Or does he or she hold a different view?

I hope that this short illustration has served to illuminate a very important factor in any competence analysis project: *never assume*! You must clarify:

- Why the competence framework is required.
- What are the plans for its future use.
- What is the agreed understanding of the term 'competence'.

An analysis project will only define what the competences are – ie, a project will produce a tool or foundation for further analysis and development

Why Do You Need A Competence Framework?

Table 1.3 provides a useful reference list to aid discussions with all stake-holders in the analysis and development project. You will find that people need encouragement to think in detail about the purpose of a planned project – focus on avoiding assumptions and achieving clarity and commonality of purpose. You need this information in order to select the correct tools and techniques for the analysis and development.

Make it clear that the development project itself will not achieve the required outcome – it will only provide the framework on which these activities can be based.

Table 1.3 *Potential uses of a competence framework*

A framework for restructuring a role
A framework for assessing/measuring performance of individuals
A framework for assessing/measuring performance of groups/teams
A framework for improving work processes
A framework for improving work procedures
A framework for conducting a skills audit
A framework for conducting a training needs analysis
A framework for completing training design
Defining the current role requirements as a precursor to any of these activities
Defining the future role requirements as a precursor to any of these activities
A framework for recruitment
A framework for career development
A framework for succession planning
A framework for a new reward system
A framework for identifying mobility of employees across the organisation
A framework for conducting training evaluation
A framework for linking internal assessment to external accreditation
A framework to define requirements for a new role or area of business

Defining Terms

As you can see, simple questions, with a few prompts, can help to define the problem in far clearer terms. The actual problem to be addressed may be any one, or a combination of the list in Table 1.3.

This discussion can help to enlighten all participants on the real potential of a competence framework – most people have a well-defined (if not well-expressed) personal view of 'competence', based on previous experience. They are often not aware of the full range of uses that this type of framework can have.

The discussion following this initial question may also (as is often the case) provide the opportunity to identify differences in opinion, in expectations and in perception among all stakeholders in the proposed analysis. This leads you nicely into your next key question.

What do we mean by competence?

It is important not to ignore this simple question. It is very easy for a project to proceed on assumptions.

'Competence' is an overworked term. If you put ten people in a room and ask them to explain their understanding of 'competence', you are likely to receive at least twelve definitions!

If you are aiming to analyse and define competences within your own organisation, it really does not matter if your organisation's definition does not conform with those of others. What is essential is that everyone involved in the development project and in the further use of the defined competences has a common understanding and expectation of:

- what is being defined
- why it is being defined
- what the resulting competences/ies will look like
- the intended uses of the competences/ies once they are defined.

These questions are incorporated into a project planning tool for you to use in Chapter 2.

Competences or competencies?

Once again, this may sound like a simple question – but one that can lead to disaster if ignored. Assumptions must be clarified and terms defined. Both these terms are used interchangeably. The generally accepted understanding of these terms is as follows:

Table 1.4 *Example of occupational competences*

UNIT	009	Make a Sales Presentation

ELEMENT 9.1   Investigate and establish customer needs and interests

Performance Criteria		Range
9.1.1	Customer requirements are identified by tactful questioning	**1 Customers** (a) existing (b) potential
9.1.2	'Buying signals' given by the customer are correctly interpreted and acted upon	**2 'Buying signals'** (a) verbal (b) non-verbal
9.1.3	Relevant product or service advantages are conveyed accurately and promptly, and matched to the customer's requirements	**3 Procedures** (a) documentary
9.1.4	Customer questions are answered with clear, accurate and relevant information	(b) timing and manner of approach (c) agreed protocols
9.1.5	Where customer requirements cannot be met the reasons are noted, analysed and acted upon appropriately	(d) legal constraints
9.1.6	Agreement is reached with the customer on the nature of his or her requirements	
9.1.7	Procedures carried out in order to establish customer needs conform with organisational and legal requirements, where appropriate	

Forms of Requirements

Suggested forms of evidence could include:

- assessors' reports detailing activities undertaken and successfully completed, eg observation of customer reaction/interaction through field accompaniment reports
- products of work, including working documents, eg product/service information/price lists used, log of needs/interests identified and log of questions/needs where specialist advice required
- witness testimony from colleagues/customers, eg letters/reports
- oral questioning – discussions prior to and following the investigation of customer needs/interests
- simulated activities which may include the candidate using skills in questioning techniques (probing customer upon needs/interests) (role play)

Additional Guidance

- Performance evidence must be provided for a least
  - ONE type of customer
- Supplementary evidence must be provided for any items of the range for which performance evidence is unavailable

Underpinning Knowledge

1	Difference of approach to existing/potential customers
2	Product/service knowledge in relation to customer needs
3	'Buying signals' and buying psychology
4	Types of business structure (sole traders, partnerships, private limited companies, cooperatives, public limited companies)
5	Reasons people buy
6	Factors that affect the buying process including competitive activity and the replacement cycle
7	Legal or regulatory constraints on the sales person
8	Selling techniques (selling up, selling on, range selling)

Sources of Evidence

- Performance evidence through observations over a period of time of the candidate's normal (naturally occurring) work activities
- Supplementary evidence to support performance and ensure full coverage of the range and underpinning knowledge and may include
  - oral questioning
  - simulated activities

9

Competences: this term usually refers to outcome-based occupational competences, such as those developed for National Vocational Qualifications (NVQs) in the UK. They define expectations of performance at work in output terms.

Competencies: this term usually refers to behavioural-based descriptors of performance. They describe the inputs which help achieve successful performance at work.

I find the simplest way to describe the difference (and thus avoid long-drawn-out debates) is:

Competences are about the work and its achievement.

Competencies are about the people who do the work.

In planning your project, you must achieve common understanding on this issue. What are people expecting to see once the analysis and development is complete? Are they expecting to see statements which define the outcomes of work (work-related competences), or are they expecting to see statements which define what people bring to work (people-related competencies)?

The decision on this issue will influence further decisions and the ultimate purpose of the framework. Assessing work-related outcomes requires a different type of assessment method and different assessment criteria from that needed for assessing behaviours!

To help you with the initial discussions at this key stage, examples of 'competences' and of 'competencies' are provided in Tables 1.4 and 1.5. Use these to illustrate the differences.

Table 1.5 *Example of competencies*

Competency area	Personal drive
Behavioural indicators	
Positive	Negative
Actively takes responsibility for achievement of personal and business targets	Needs to be reminded repeatedly of personal and business goals and targets
Communicates and promotes team goals	Works in isolation from immediate team
Adopts an open and honest approach seeking advice and support when needed	Has difficulty accepting own limitations
Shares ideas to develop team achievement	Focuses on own goals and personal development

Functions, roles, jobs, tasks, skills, and process and procedure

Here is another potential minefield of assumptions and overused terms. Generally accepted definitions follow. However, remember that if you are analysing and developing competences/ies for your own organisation, it is *your agreed definition* that really matters – this may differ from those overleaf.

As you can begin to see, a clear understanding of terms, within your own context, is critical to the success of your analysis and development. Your stakeholders might agree that what is really needed is a task analysis – but for specific reasons, the results of this analysis will be called 'competences'. On the other hand, your stakeholders may want to be in line with external expectations and demands and be more rigid over the definitions used.

What is important from your perspective is that you know what you are expected to develop, why you are expected to develop it and the basis on which this development takes place.

What Skills Do You Need?

Analysts working on people performance must have certain practised skills (note that these are skills and not competences/ies). These might include any combination of:

Observation
Questioning
Analytical thinking
Data collection
Questionnaire design
Patience
Attention to detail
Summarising complex ideas and data
Feedback
Group facilitation
Interviewing

All of these skills apply when using the collection of tools and techniques in this book. You may need to learn some new skills, or develop some existing ones.

Chapter 2 helps you select skills to accompany the tools and techniques. This skill selection will help you to ensure that the right people, with the right skills, undertake the analysis and development of your competence framework.

Function: The purpose of a work activity or a broad area of work activity.

Examples: (purpose of activity – used within development of NVQs in the UK)

    (a) Produce word-processed documents using a range of software applications.

    (b) Design promotional materials to meet needs of defined market segment.

Examples: (broad area of work activity – often used for behavioural competencies)

    (a) Administration support.

    (b) Marketing.

Role: An area of work activity within an organisation undertaken by specified groups.

Examples:

    (a) Production line operators.

    (b) Supervisors.

Job: A defined area of work relating to one job holder, or to a number of individuals who undertake identical work activities.

Examples:

    (a) Production line operator (filling).

    (b) Production supervisors.

Task: A single component of a work activity or a job.

Examples:

    (a) Prepare line for filling process.

    (b) Complete production reports.

Skills: Acquired abilities which are applied to work activities.

Examples:

    (a) Analytical thinking.

    (b) Interpersonal communication.

Process: The stages of work activity.

Examples:

    (a) Prepare work area.

    (b) Test equipment.

    (c) Complete work.

    (d) Record outcome.

Procedure: Specified requirements for each stage of work activity.

Examples:

To prepare work area:

    (a) Identify correct equipment and materials.

    (b) Position equipment with regard to safety requirements.

Are You Ready to Begin Planning?

Check that you are ready to make a start. Do you know:

1. Why competencies/ies need to be developed?
2. The plans/expectations for use of the competences/ies?
3. For whom the competences/ies are to be developed?
4. Whether the competences/ies are to reflect current or future expectations?
5. Whether you are aiming to produce competences or competencies?
6. Whether there is a common understanding of the concept of competence
   (a) across the organisation
   (b) among all members of the project team
   (c) among those for whom competences/ies are to be developed?
7. Whether the project has the support (and understanding) of key stakeholders?
8. Whether concepts of function, role, task, job and skill are commonly understood?
9. Whether competences/ies are to be defined as workrelated or people related?

If you can provide a clear and positive answer to all these questions, then you are ready to move on to Chapter 2 and to work on planning the detail of your project, including the selection of relevant tools and techniques.

If not – you have some more discussion and clarification to do!

2 Planning Your Analysis

Outline Plan

Complete this outline as your key reference document.

1. Competence/ies need to be developed in order to:	
2. Expectations for use(s) of the competence/ies are:	
3. Competence/ies are to be developed for these target groups:	
4. Competence/ies are required to reflect performance needed (circle correct response)	Currently In the future
5. The purpose of the project is to produce outcome-based competences OR The purpose of the project is to produce behaviour-based competencies	YES/NO YES/NO
6. There is a common understanding of the meaning of competence among: (a) the project management group (b) the target group (c) the organisation	 YES/NO YES/NO YES/NO
7. Key stakeholders in this project are:	
8. Key stakeholders have a common understanding of the meaning of competence	YES/NO

Three steps of analysis

The purpose of analysis is to identify the component parts of a prede-fined 'whole'. The 'whole' may be a function, a job or a role (see Chapter 1 for definitions).

Identifying components, however, is only one step in the analysis process. Once identified, it is important to discover the relationship between the components and then restructure them in a format which meets the purpose of the analysis (see Figure 2.1).

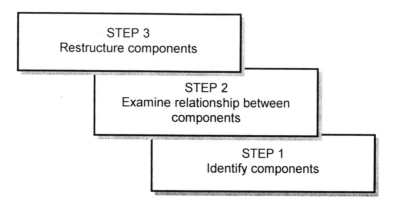

STEP 3
Restructure components

STEP 2
Examine relationship between
components

STEP 1
Identify components

Figure 2.1 *Three steps of analysis*

Fit for purpose

How you go about taking these steps depends upon the main purpose of your project. If you have clearly defined points 1 and 2 on the outline plan at the beginning of this chapter, you will be ready to begin the selection of the correct tools and techniques.

Selecting Your Tools and Techniques

The following tables help you to select the right tools for your project. You will need more than one tool. No single tool or technique will cover all three steps: you will always need at least one tool from the 'Step One' box shown in Table 2.1.

You may use one tool for breaking down the job/role/function into its component parts, and perhaps a second for specifying the interrelation-ship of these components and for structuring. You may even find the use of two or three tools for the first step is helpful.

Table 2.1 *Selecting tools and techniques*

	Key questions	Possible tools and techniques
Step One **Identifying components**	What is the job/role/function? (you will always need at least one tool from this section)	Functional analysis Job function technique Walk and talk technique Card sort (dacum) technique Interview note technique Daily log technique Task matrix technique List expansion technique
Steps Two and Three **Examine relationships**	How is it done?	Process chart Risk assessment Man-machine chart Flow chart Operation chart Stimulus-response Decision technique Critical path analysis
Step Three **Restructure components**	How can it be improved?	Performance probe Behaviour counting Matrix technique Problem analysis Repertory grids
	How can it be learned?	Critical incident analysis Fault tree Imagination technique Guided training aid

When completing steps two and three you will also need to ensure that you select tools which will produce the right *kind* of information. For example, if the intended purpose of a competence framework is for use in training needs analysis, you will wish to ensure that you select tools from the 'How can it be learned?' section, when restructuring your components. If the framework is to be used to *improve* the job/role/function, you will select from the 'How can it be improved?' section.

The following table can be used as an alternative reference point when selecting tools and techniques for steps two and three. As you become more familiar with each of the tools and techniques listed, you will be able to experiment with new combinations and modifications to meet your intended purpose. Table 2.2 is a guide for readers who are new to competence analysis and/or unfamiliar with the tools and techniques included in this book.

Table 2.2 *Matching tools to intended use of competences/ies*

Intended use of competence framework	Use of tools and techniques from the section for:
Restructuring	What is the job/role/function?
Training Design	How can it be learned? How can it be improved?
Procedures/Work Instructions	How is it done? How can it be improved?
Processes	How is it done?
Skills Audit	How is it done? How can it be learned?

Scoping the Analysis

Once you have completed your outline plan and selected your tools and techniques, you should finalise the scope and outcomes of your analysis and development project.

The proforma in Figure 2.2 provides you with the key headings for your agreement and plan; here's a guide to using it.

Overview: note why the project is necessary, the intended use of the competences to be developed and the key users (short and long term).

Agreed Definition of Competence: note, as agreed in planning stage.

Goal of Project: note overall aim (see Chapter 1 for guidance).

Objectives of Project: note overall objectives (see Chapter 1 for guidance).

Resources: note people, finance, accommodation (workshops, interviews).

Management: note project manager, team reporting lines, responsibilities.

Products/Outcomes: note agreed expectations, eg competences or competencies, format, style, content.

Evaluation: note methods agreed for:

    (a)   evaluating outcomes of analysis/development
    (b)   long-term evaluation of use of competence framework.

Tools and Techniques: note tools/techniques selected for each step of analysis.

Figure 2.2 *Agreement and plan proforma*

3

Tools and Techniques

This section provides details on each individual analysis tool and technique. Information is provided in the following format.

- when to use this tool/technique
- how to use this tool/technique
- advantages and disadvantages of its use.

Use the tables on pages 17 and 18 to select the tools you need, complete your agreement and plan (page 19). You are now ready to apply your selected tools to complete your analysis and development of competences/ies.

Tools and techniques are included in the following order:

Section 3.1: Identifying Components
Functional Analysis
Job Function
Walk and Talk
Card Sort
Interview Note
Daily Log
Task Matrix
List Expansion

Section 3.2: Examining Relationships
Process Chart
Risk Assessment
Man-Machine Chart
Flow Chart
Operation Chart
Stimulus and Response

Decision Technique
Critical Path Analysis

Section 3.3: Restructuring Components

3.3.1: Improving
Performance Probe
Behaviour Counting
Matrix Technique
Problem Analysis
Repertory Grids

3.3.2: Learning
Critical Incident Analysis
Fault Tree
Imagination Technique
Guided Training Aid

3.1 Identifying Components

Functional Analysis Technique

Job Function Technique

Walk and Talk Technique

Card Sort Technique

Interview Note Technique

Daily Log Technique

Task Matrix Technique

List Expansion Technique

Functional analysis

When to use functional analysis

You will use functional analysis to provide a basis for identifying components of competence when:

- working with generic roles (eg, management, sales)
- conducting an organisation-wide analysis
- aiming to identify cross-functional competences/ies
- developing competences for National Vocational Qualifications (NVQs)
- aiming to develop in-company competences in NVQ format.

How to use functional analysis

Functional analysis is a general term for the identification of component 'functions' which contribute to the achievement of a 'key purpose'. It is important to clarify that the 'functions' referred to in this technique are divorced from both the people who undertake the work and the business department or division in which the functions operate.

Many business organisations distinguish functions by the type of product or service. For example, a motor manufacturer may have business 'functions' relating to:

Executive car production
Saloon/family car production
Sports car production

This not the categorisation of 'functions' you are seeking to establish. Many work activities within the above business functions are identical – but simply focused on a different product.

Remember, at this point, you are not concerned with the different skills or knowledge brought to these work activities. Your main aim will be to define the required outcomes of activities.

We might therefore think of the functional analysis approach as one which 'unpacks' everything which must be achieved in order that a business organisation achieves its purpose and objectives. Figure 3.1 illustrates this.

By breaking down an organisation's key purpose in this way, we identify all *functions* which are essential to success. We then use these functions (often called a functional map) as the basis for the development of competences or competencies (see page 8).

The identified functions can themselves be used as a basis for restructuring roles and for planning other HR functions.

If we follow the functional analysis route used in the development of NVQs, then we also identify occupational standards of performance (or competences). This development process, known as 'analysis by function', is illustrated later in this section.

FUNCTION

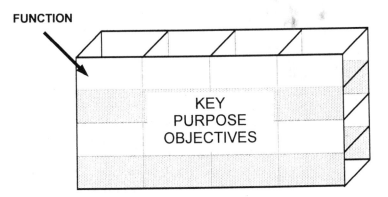

KEY
PURPOSE
OBJECTIVES

Figure 3.1 *Functional analysis approach*

Planning your functional analysis

You will need to conduct a number of workshops. In preparation for these workshops, you will need to conduct some organisation research. Begin by identifying the following. Collect relevant reports, plans, organograms, job descriptions.

- Organisation mission, vision and objectives
- Planned change
- Organogram, structure charts
- HR strategy
- Current appraisal/assessment system
- Current career development structure
- Current succession planning system
- Current grading and job evaluation systems
- Current quality systems and procedures
- Other current and planned development projects.

You will need to collect this information across the area in which you plan to conduct the analysis. If this is to be organisation-wide, then you have a lot of research to do. If it is for one operating division, or for one generic role (eg, marketing) then your workload will be less.

All the above information influences the effectiveness of your analysis, both in terms of its process and outcomes. You must have a clear picture of current systems, processes and procedures *as well as* future plans *and* any other projects/initiatives under way.

Once you have researched and summarised this information, you can plan your workshops.

Your first workshop must be with Senior Managers. The purpose of this workshop is to define and agree a 'key purpose statement' which spans the full scope of your analysis. You will also use this workshop to define essential functions which, collectively, achieve the key purpose.

The same approach is then adopted for each of the key functions identified. The result of all this activity is a functional map. This forms the basis for further work. The tools you will use in these further stages will depend upon the aim of your analysis (see page 15). If your aim is to produce competencies in the format of NVQs, see page 29.

Step one – functional analysis

In this first exercise, you will identify the *key purpose* and *key functions* of the business function/roles on which you are focusing your development. You will also begin to identify some of the *qualities* of these functions which contribute to measuring successful achievement:

First, define the business function/area:

We are aiming to develop competencies for: ....

....

....

Now consider the *key purpose* of this function/area. This key purpose should be prepared as an active statement and should clearly express why this function/area exists – what is its overall aim? Keep in mind the contribution of the function/area to overall business objectives.

Your key purpose statement should be based on all of the following:

Business objectives	Customers	Commitments
Values	Quality	Milestones
Culture	Targets	Markets

A key purpose statement should:

- encompass the entire function/area for which you are developing competencies
- be an active statement – begin with a verb
- define the business domain and why it is attractive to customers
- include an aim for competitive advantage
- reference values which reinforce business strategy/objectives
- reflect the organisation culture
- provide a reference point for the development of competencies.

This probably sounds like a pretty tall order! Remember that this key purpose, once defined, is for use as a development tool – you are not aiming to prepare a catchy phrase for promotional purposes. It is more important to capture all of the above as a reference guide, and thus have a longer key purpose statement, than it is to achieve a short but insufficient result. Figure 3.2 provides an example.

The key purpose of a hotel chain property management function:

Active verb	Object	Conditions/Context
Achieve	the number one public rating in the European hotel industry	through development, management and continuous improvement of the quality of accommodation

Figure 3.2 *Example of a key purpose statement*

Having achieved consensus on a working key purpose statement, we now need to explore how this breaks down into *key functions*. This will help us identify what you *need to happen* within your function/area in order to ensure that competencies include a contribution to business objectives and encompass culture, values and a people focus.

Think of your key purpose as a jigsaw – to complete the full picture we need to have all the pieces. Each key function is one jigsaw piece. Key functions take the same form as the key purpose and each should represent a discrete contribution to the big picture; see Figure 3.3.

Key functions can be defined at various levels of operation – we could continue the process right down to job-specific tasks. However, the objective of this development process is to identify individual functions at a level which:

- represents achievement of a measurable outcome
- is discrete from other key functions
- contributes to higher-level functions.

We can therefore think of this process as a mapping exercise – one which identifies key outcomes at various levels, each linking back to a higher level function. The 'knack' in this process is knowing when to stop!

The key functions of a hotel chain property management:

Active verb	Object	Conditions/Context
Research and improve	the quality of accommodation and related services	to attract and retain a higher volume of European customers
Market	services and image	to European customers
Support	hotel management	in the identification and resolution of factors influencing highest quality accommodation and services

Figure 3.3 *Example of a list of key functions*

Use the proforma in Figure 3.4 to note what you feel are key functions which contribute to the key purpose you have agreed. At this stage, do not worry about the level these functions represent – these can be discussed further to clarify and resolve a final 'map'.

Now we have agreed a basic function list, we can examine some of the more qualitative aspects of these. Make a list of what you feel to be the key qualities you would look for if you were assessing successful achievement of the stated functions; an example is given in Figure 3.5.

The first step of our development process is now complete. We can move on to step two.

Key functions – my ideas

Active verb	Object	Conditions/Context

Following discussion with your facilitator and agreement with the group, note below the key functions you have agreed.

Key functions – consensus view

Active verb	Object	Conditions/Context

Figure 3.4 *A proforma for key functions*

Key Function (as agreed)	Qualities I would seek if assessing successful achievement
Support hotel management in the identification and resolution of factors influencing highest quality accommodation and services	*Accurate* identification of factors *Innovative* and *cost-effective* solutions *Consistency* and *sensitivity* in support *Open* and *honest* communication

Figure 3.5 *Measuring quality of outcomes – an example*

Step two – developing NVQs
(See example of NVQ competence, page 9.)

If the aim of your analysis is to produce NVQs, or competences in NVQ format, you will take your functional analysis a step further. This involves taking the functions you have identified and breaking them down to a lower level (known as 'disaggregation to element level' – see analysis by function, technical guidance, DfEE and Training Agency 1996).

Once this 'element' level has been identified, a further step identifies 'performance criteria'. You then return to your earlier research material to identify the 'range statement' and 'knowledge and understanding'.

The following provides a brief overview of this process. Detailed guidance can be found in materials produced by the DfEE/Training Agency, as referenced above.

Identifying elements of competence   Elements of competence are identified through using the same process of functional analysis. Take the functions you have identified and ask, 'What has to happen to achieve this?'

The statements resulting from this analysis should continue following the same format:

> verb   object   condition/context

The difficulty is knowing when to stop! The best way to familiarise yourself with the process is to examine various element titles in current NVQs – preferably the latest approved versions. You will see that these statements reflect outcomes of activities and not tasks.

Developing performance criteria   Once elements are defined, you can establish performance criteria. Once again, a workshop approach is best. Participants in these workshops should include a representative sample of role-holders – people whose work activities include the elements you are including in the workshop.

The simplest approach is to take each element in turn and ask:

- What are the critical outcomes of this activity?
- What are the key qualities of these outcomes?
- Are any aspects of the process critical to performance?

For example, let's take an element such as: Shampoo client's hair.

- What are the critical outcomes of this activity?
  (a) the client
  (b) the client's hair
- What are the key qualities of these outcomes?
  Client – comfortable, satisfied
  Client's hair – clean, free from shampoo and other agents, ready for next stage.

With this information, we can prepare performance criteria in NVQ format. This means each performance criterion starts with the critical outcome, followed by the qualities of that outcome. For example:

Element: Shampoo client's hair

Performance criteria:

- the client is comfortable, and has no complaints
- the client's hair is clean, free from cleansing or other agents, with excess moisture removed
- the client is ready for the next stage of service.

Note that all criteria are presented in the *current* tense.

The final question: 'Are there any aspects of the process which are critical to performance?' This ensures that assessment of competence will focus on the important aspects of competent performance – this will include all aspects of quality, hygiene or safety, and those for which cost of failure would be high. Only these *critical* aspects should be included. For example, a criterion to add to our example above might be:

- only sterilised tools and equipment are used.

Defining range and knowledge Referring back to your previous research materials and any existing training materials will help you define range and knowledge.

The range statement should:

- cover all contexts and conditions in which the *element* must be assessed for competent performance
- relate directly to performance criteria.

For example, the performance criteria refer to 'clients'. What type of clients should be included in the range? If the role-holder is competent, will they be able to shampoo hair for clients of all ages; those who are regular or casual customers; those who have allergies? Will they be able to shampoo hair which is short, long, coloured, bleached, permed, fine, thick?

By defining the range in this way, you are effectively setting the *scope* of competent performance. It is essential to get this right, or the resulting assessment system will be unfair.

Your range statement will then provide the basis to scope the knowledge and understanding which underpins competent performance.

See page 9 for an example of a completed occupational competence in NVQ format.

Advantages and disadvantages

Advantages

This technique allows you to examine work roles in a new way. It encourages role-holders to consider their role in depth, and in terms of outcomes/achievements. The workshop approach improves communication channels across departments and helps employees to understand more about the broader context in which they work. The process builds on top-down commitment, and links performance to organisation objectives.

Disadvantages

The workshop and research approach can be time- and resource-intensive. Top-down commitment and understanding can be difficult to achieve.

Job Function Technique

When to use job function technique

This technique is useful when analysing jobs. Use this technique if you want to break a job down into its component tasks. Although the correct name for this technique is 'job function', what is actually identified in the first instance are 'skills', using our definitions on page 11.

How to use the job function technique

You might use workshops with a group of job-holders or individual interviews. 'Master performers' (those considered to be excellent in their job) are usually those included in these workshops or interviews.

You should review jobs to identify the key skills (see page 11 and Functional analysis).

Identify information, context and people related to each function.

Identify specific actions to be performed, and write task statements.

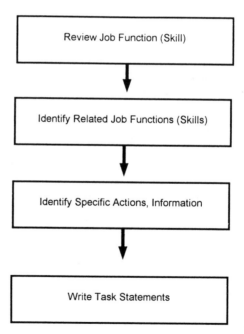

Figure 3.6 *Job function technique*

Your resulting analysis will look something like this example, based on a production operator:

Job function (skills)	Description
Calculating	Performing arithmetic operations to plan, check or compare progress
Analysing	Examine, check and evaluate information using standard procedures and guidelines.
Coordinating	Set standards, goals and objectives. Plan sequence of activities, monitor progress, prioritise action, plan and implement change to achieve goals.
Operating	Perform sequence of actions, in accordance with procedures to achieve production results
	Task statements
Calculating	receive standards and output requirements calculate setting to achieve specification calculate adjustments to improve progress
Analysing	

Advantages and disadvantages

Advantages
Defining tasks can be more effective when based on a broader initial analysis. For jobs at skilled and semi-skilled levels, this can be a useful approach.

Disadvantages
The skill-based nature of this technique means the analysis can focus on input and process (ie, *what* the individual *brings* to the task and *how* the task is conducted) and ignores outcomes (*why* the task is completed). This approach is really best, therefore, when used when 'competences' are equated with 'skills and tasks'.

Walk and Talk Technique

When to use the walk and talk technique

This technique is used to identify the activities, materials, sequence of work and timing of tasks, usually for skilled, semi-skilled jobs.

How to use the walk and talk technique

As its name suggests, this technique involves the analyst shadowing a 'master performer' and recording all aspects of work activity. The master performer talks through each action and defines materials, tools and equipment used. The analyst records all information.

This technique is often used in conjunction with the Interview Note Technique, the List Expansion Technique or the Task Matrix Technique.

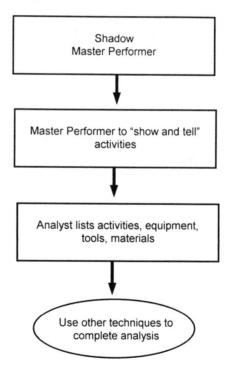

Figure 3.7 *Walk and talk technique*

Your completed list might look something like this:

Task list	Equipment/tools/materials list
Locate	pH Meter
Operate	Centrifuge
Calibrate	Microscope
Diagnose	Autoclave
Analyse	Viscometer
	Automatic Titrator
	Hydrometer

Note again – what is referred to as 'task' in this technique might equate to 'function' in another technique (using textbook terminology). This does not matter, as long as you have agreed understanding and well-defined terms for your analysis (see page 8).

Once this analysis technique has been applied – a further tool (see above) would be used to complete the analysis. See relevant sections for appropriate tools as noted above.

Advantages and disadvantages

Advantages

If what you need is a basis on which to examine effective use of tools, equipment, etc, this technique is simple and can be conducted within a short timescale if a small sample of master performers is selected.

Disadvantages

For highly skilled technical roles this can be a time-consuming technique as coverage of *all* tools and equipment is required.

Card Sort Technique

When to use the card sort technique

This technique is often used to identify process, or to establish work instructions, such as those used in ISO 9000. It is task based. Using this technique can be a precursor to setting performance criteria (see page 30). The technique is often used when time or resources are limited, as analysis is conducted from relevant documentation.

How to use the card sort technique

- Collect job descriptions, work instructions and training materials relevant to area/scope of analysis.
- Review all documentation and record all task statements identified.
- Record each task statement on a separate card.

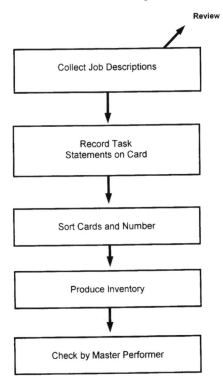

Figure 3.8 *Card sort technique*

- Sort the cards into a logical, sequential order.
- Number recorded tasks sequentially.
- Produce task statements in a task inventory.
- Have master performer review the task inventory for accuracy, sequence and relevance.
- Revise task statements as appropriate.

Definition of tasks

For this technique a 'task' is a statement such as:

> Job: Fast Food Cook
> Prepare deep fat fryer
> Cook chicken
> Cook chipped potatoes
> Package meal
> Clean cooking area.

Each of these have sub-tasks relating to the sequence of activities. When sorted and numbered your task list will look something like this.

1. Prepare deep fat fryer
   1.1 add cooking oil
   1.2 heat cooking oil
   1.3 monitor oil temperature.
2. Cook chicken
   2.1 remove chicken from storage
   2.2 thaw frozen chicken
   2.3 batter chicken
   2.4 place chicken in cooking oil
   2.5 monitor cooking
   2.6 test chicken for completion of cooking
   2.7 remove chicken from cooking oil.

Advantages and disadvantages

Advantages

This technique requires only the analyst and a master performer. It can be completed in a short timescale, for single jobs requiring a task-based analysis as the foundation for development of competences.

Disadvantages

This approach can be subjective. For complex jobs it can also be time consuming for the analyst. Interviews may also be required to test results. It is best conducted by a specialist who has knowledge of the job, which requires time away from normal work activity.

Interview Note Technique

When to use the interview technique

Use this technique if you need to adopt an approach which involves individual interviews and if you are aiming to identify key tasks of a job or role.

How to use the interview note technique

Identify 'master performers' – those who are considered to be excellent in their job/role. The process for this technique is illustrated in Figure 3.9. As you determine if each main duty needs to be detailed, consider the following rules. If you decide to stop at a particular level of detail, note your reasons for doing so.

Rule 1   Continue adding detail until sufficient to meet the situation's objectives.

Rule 2   Continue adding detail to very difficult and critical tasks – consider the cost of failure as a key criterion.

Rule 3   Continue adding detail until an intermediate level is reached – avoid making your statements too general.

Rule 4   Err on the side of too little detail unless it is very expensive to reanalyse the tasks.

Your completed analysis sheet will look something like that shown on page 41. In this example, five duties were identified. Only duties numbers 1 and 4 were detailed. Duty 1 was found to involve five sub-tasks, one of which required further detailing.

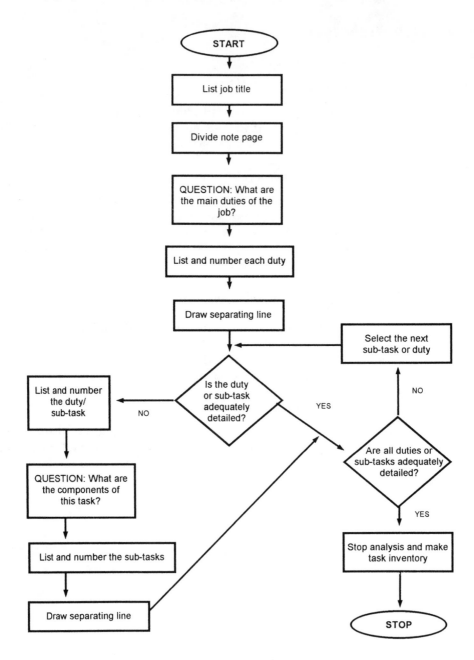

Figure 3.9 *Interview note technique*

Example interview note completed

Number	Task statement	Reason analysis stopped
1	File documents	1 Continue analysis
2	Greet visitors	2,3 Stop analysis since tasks
3	Answer telephone	are very easy
4	Maintain office supplies	4 Continue analysis
5	Type letters	5 Stop analysis since secretary is expert typist
1	File documents	
1.1	Determine document topic	1.1 Continue analysis
1.2	Fill out subject card(s)	1.2 to 1.5 Stop analysis,
1.3	Assign document number	secretary will learn these
1.4	Place document in file drawer	tasks by being shown one
1.5	Place subject card(s) in card file	time
1.1	Determine document topic	
1.1.1	Read document title	1.1.1 to 1.1.3 Stop analysis
1.1.2	Read document introduction	since further analysis
1.1.3	Read document summary	concerns how to read
4.	Maintain office supplies	4.1 Stop, checklist easily
4.1	Complete required materials checklist	understood
4.2	Order supplies	4.2 Stop, easy checklist

After notes are taken, rewrite your notes as task statements to form a task inventory which will look like the following:

    1.0 File documents
    1.1 Determine document type
        1.1.1 Read document title
        1.1.2 Read document introduction
        1.1.3 Read document summary
    1.2 Fill in subject card(s)
    1.3 Assign document number
    1.4 Place document in file drawer
    1.5 Place subject card(s) in card file
    2.0 Greet visitors
    3.0 Answer telephone
    4.0 Maintain office supplies
    4.1 Complete required materials checklist
    4.2 Order necessary supplies
    5.0 Type letters.

Advantages and disadvantages

Advantages

If your analysis is for a small group of fairly task-based, low-level activities, this will be useful for identifying key tasks/activities. The one-to-one approach is also helpful in encouraging people to take ownership of competences in their work by involving them fully in the analysis process.

Disadvantages

The above example was taken from some early work in this field. I selected it specifically to illustrate the possible inconsistency of this approach. Decisions regarding when to stop the analysis can be very subjective. This technique is also very time consuming.

Daily Log Technique

When to use the daily log technique

Use this technique to determine task statements when there is no existing job description, or when creating a new job description/job.

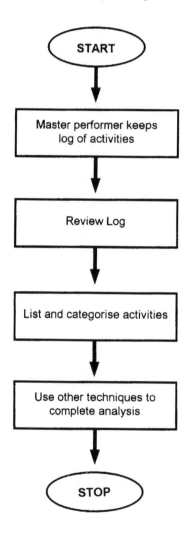

Figure 3.10 *Daily log technique*

How to use the daily log technique

This involves considering the job on a day-to-day basis, either by shadowing someone who is doing it, asking a current job holder to maintain a 'log', or working through the (new) job as a testbed. The technique is illustrated in Figure 3.10.

A daily log of activities over a set period of time needs to be kept, recording activities, times and explanations. The log should be kept until all major tasks have been completed at least once. Review and categorisation provide a list of all key activities and objects. A daily log for a training manager would look like this:

Daily log for a manager		
Time	*Activity*	*Explanation*
8.00–8.30	*Requested* and *submitted* daily *time cards*.	I *called* to *remind* two employees to complete their time cards. I *reviewed* each time card to ensure it was correct, *recorded overtime* and *absence* in the record book, and sent the *cards* to payroll.
	Answered telephone call.	Request from marketing department for attendance at meeting. Discussed and diarised.
8.30–9.00	*Read mail* from previous day.	*Wrote* short *messages* on some of the mail encouraging different types of *action* and *routed* it to various *individuals.* Placed several service descriptions in the 'to be filed' *drawer*. *Discarded* several others.
9.00–10.30	*Met* with personnel *manager*.	*Discussed* various *alternatives* for a staff training programme. *Decided* on three *alternatives*.
10.30–11.00	*Met* with training *analyst*.	*Discussed* a *needs assessment* that was being done and *suggested* several *ways* that it might proceed.
11.00–12.00	*Wrote* a *justification* for contracting out the evaluation of the training	The writing involved the *review* of several related *documents* and one *phone call* to the *bid processor*.

This technique should be followed up by use of one of the following:

> Interview note technique
> Card sort technique
> Task matrix technique
> List expansion technique

Advantages and disadvantages

Advantages

This technique involves people fully in the analysis and can provide a detailed review.

Disadvantages

Shadowing a job-holder can create tension. Asking a job-holder to record activities can be a very subjective approach.

Task Matrix Technique

When to use the task matrix technique

This is a useful tool for organising actions performed within a job/role in order that job-holders can easily identify task statements. It works best with low level tasks when a few basic actions are performed with various people or types of equipment.

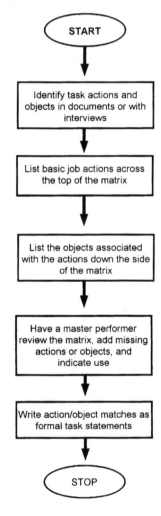

Figure 3.11 *Task matrix technique*

How to use the task matrix technique

You will need to format task statements into a comprehensive matrix, as detailed in Figure 3.11.

Review all job-related documents (descriptions, structure charts, training guides, etc). Identify all actions performed and all objects acted upon. (You might also use the card sort technique for this.)

Categorise all identified actions, eliminate those which are redundant. List those remaining across the top of a matrix sheet. There will usually be fewer actions than objects.

List all objects associated with the actions down the side of the matrix. For example, management jobs will include people, paper, computers, materials, office supplies. Operator jobs will include long lists of equipment and tools.

Review the completed matrix with job-holders and add any important actions and objects felt to be necessary. If the action does not apply to a listed object it should be left blank. All matches between actions and objects should be checked.

Rewrite the action/object pairs as a formal task inventory. A completed matrix will look similar to the one shown in Figure 3.12.

EQUIPMENT	LOCATE	OPERATE	ADJUST	REPAIR
1. Trickling Filters				X
2. First-stage Clarifiers				X
3. Feeding and Transfer System			X	X

Figure 3.12 *Example task matrix*

Advantages and disadvantages

Advantages

This is a useful way to involve job-holders in the analysis: individuals can undertake the first analysis and produce the draft matrix themselves. The analyst will then review.

Disadvantages

This is specifically task-based and will not adapt well to use at a higher level of generality.

List Expansion Technique

When to use the list expansion technique

Use this technique to structure interview or questionnaire data. This is useful when the jobs/roles for analysis involve many or complex actions and numerous types of equipment/tools etc.

How to use the list expansion technique

The flow chart in Figure 3.13 illustrates the process. Once again, the analyst must start with a review of relevant job-related documents.

The analyst must format task statements into comprehensive lists, beginning with the job-related documents. All actions and objects must be identified and categorised. The Card Sort Technique would be helpful at this stage.

The analyst should then detail all actions and list them under the appropriate object before reviewing these with a job-holder and asking the following questions for each action and each object respectively:

1. What related equipment/tools/materials are used for this action?
2. What other actions are performed in relation to this object?

Once completed, the actions and objects are rewritten as formal task statements if this format is needed for further use; often this is not necessary.

Advantages and disadvantages

Advantages
The main advantage of this technique over the Task Matrix Technique is that the addition of objects and actions in each category is somewhat simpler to undertake. The list expansion technique produces task statements which can be used without further rewriting (see example task statements in Interview Note Technique).

Disadvantages
All relevant documentation must be available – this is not always possible. There is less standardisation across tasks with this technique than with the Task Matrix Technique so it is best used in contexts where there are multiple actions/objects.

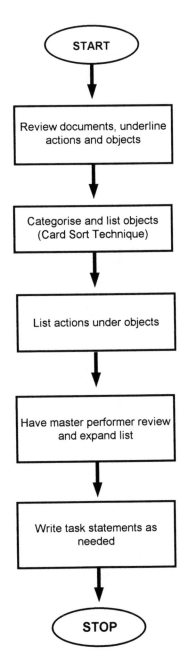

Figure 3.13 *List expansion technique*

3.2 Examining Relationships

Process Chart

Risk Assessment Technique

Man-Machine Chart

Flow Chart Technique

Operation Chart

Stimulus and Response

Decision Technique

Critical Path Analysis

Process Chart

When to use the process chart

This technique is used to record and categorise the steps in a task. Five basic task categories are used to give a fairly simple description of the task. From the finished chart, improvements can be made to the process. The technique is illustrated in Figure 3.14.

How to use the process chart

The analyst categorises and records the basic process which the master performer uses when doing the task.

1. Design the process chart to match the type of task being analysed. A process chart always has chart symbols and a process description. It may also include time, distance, group-work, and summary sections.

    Process chart symbols are used during data collection as shorthand for categorising and recording the steps in the task. The symbols are shown in Figure 3.15 (page 54).
2. Observe and record the performance. Each chart is identified first, then the process description is completed. The symbols are identified and sequenced with a correcting line and the process description is either a short task statement giving indication of where transportation or storage is, or a description of inspection standard.
3. Observe and record other needed information. Several observations may be required to ensure that the process is correctly described, and to add details like distances moved or time used.
4. Combine process charts when different individuals give input to the process.
5. Summarise the process chart. The summary should include the number of operations, transportations, inspections, and delays, as well as other data, ie, total distance travelled, and total time used After the summary is complete, the task can be analysed and restructured, eliminating unneeded travel or delay.

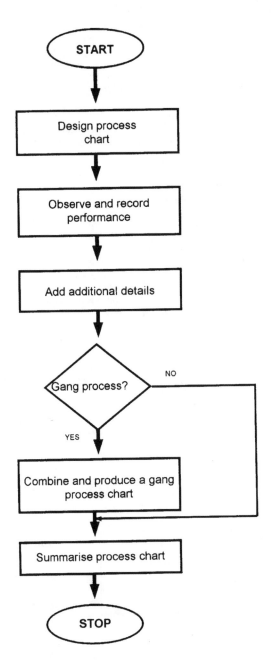

Figure 3.14 *Process chart technique*

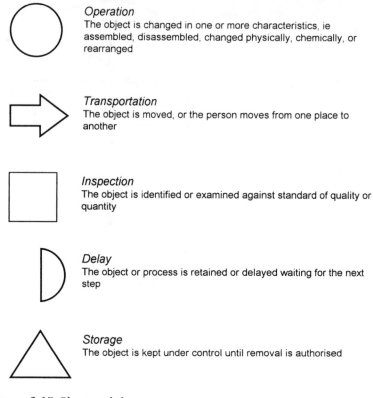

Operation
The object is changed in one or more characteristics, ie assembled, disassembled, changed physically, chemically, or rearranged

Transportation
The object is moved, or the person moves from one place to another

Inspection
The object is identified or examined against standard of quality or quantity

Delay
The object or process is retained or delayed waiting for the next step

Storage
The object is kept under control until removal is authorised

Figure 3.15 *Chart symbols*

The examples given in Figures 3.16–19 illustrate the use of this technique in several contexts.

DISTANCE IN FEET	TIME IN MINUTES	CHART SYMBOL	PROCESS DESCRIPTION
	15	● → ■ ❯ ▼	First Step
10	1	● → ■ ❯ ▼	Second Step
	5	● → ■ ❯ ▼	Third Step
	2	● → ■ ❯ ▼	Fourth Step

Figure 3.16 *Individual process chart format*

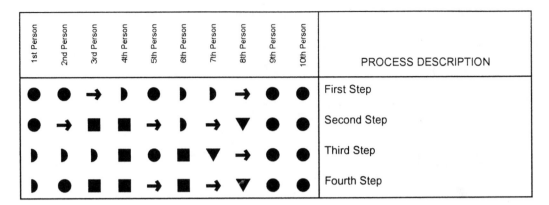

Figure 3.17 *Gang process chart format*

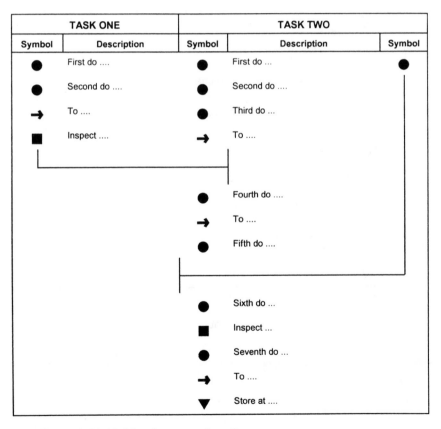

Figure 3.18 *Multi-task process chart format*

SUBJECT:	Completion of training attendance form
BEGINNING POINT:	Instructor starts one-day course
ENDING POINT:	Instructor submits records for filing
DATE:	8 December 1996

CHART SYMBOLS	PROCESS DESCRIPTION
●	Course name and date written by instructor
→	to student
●	student signs name
→	to next student
●	next student signs name
◗	Previous two steps continue until all 14 students have signed on back desk
■	instructor collects attendance sheet and examines
●	instructor signs approval
◗	waits for other records and test grades
→	to file clerk
▼	form filed

SUMMARY: Includes all 14 students

●	Operations	16
→	Transportations	15
■	Inspections	1
◗	Delays	2
▼	Storages	1

Figure 3.19 *Attendance form process chart*

Advantages and disadvantages

Advantages

The Process Chart Technique has two principal advantages: (1) the information is recorded in a short, concise manner and (2) the steps are categorised so needed improvements can be identified. Also, when workers interact on the job, their activities can be recorded on the same chart. This technique is useful for improving jobs where routing and travel time are critical.

Disadvantages

Complex decisions and groups are not easily recorded with the Process Chart Technique. It is best for basic, linear tasks like those found in assembly line jobs.

Risk Assessment Technique

When to use the risk assessment technique

This is most often used after an activity inventory, to determine the importance and difficulty of each work activity. From this assessment, further activities can be identified for more in-depth analysis and/or training. The technique is illustrated in Figure 3.20.

How to use the risk assessment technique

The analyst must work with job-holders to identify ratings of activity criticality. The two most important rating factors are *difficulty* and *importance*.

Difficulty factor

This assesses the chance of performance error by asking the following question:

> What is the possibility of inadequate performance from the average employee?

The difficulty factor can be scored in the following way:

1. Very low – very little chance of error, among the easiest 10 per cent of all activities/activities
2. Low – little chance of error, easier than average but not among the easiest; easier than seven out of ten activities.
3. Moderate – some chance of error, difficulty is average.
4. High – error is likely, harder than average but not among the most difficult; more difficult than seven out of ten activities.
5. Very high – error almost certain, harder than 90 per cent of all activities.

Importance factor

This factor assumes that performance error has a high cost of failure. The question to ask is:

> What is the cost to safety, lost revenue and public relations if the activity is performed inadequately?

The importance factor can be rated in the following way:

1. Very low – inadequate performance makes almost no difference.
2. Low – inadequate performance has undesirable public relations consequences, but the effects are not too costly, and are not unsafe.

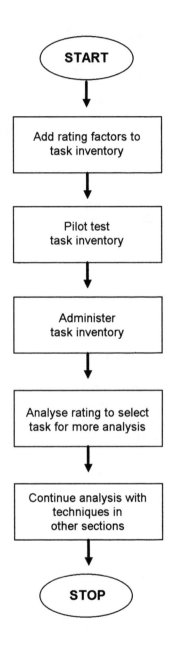

Figure 3.20 *Risk assessment technique*

3. Moderate – inadequate performance has serious public relations consequences which are very costly and are quite dangerous.
4. High – inadequate performance has severe public relations consequences which are very costly, and are quite dangerous.
5. Very high – inadequate performance has extremely severe public relations consequences which are enormously time consuming or costly, and are very dangerous.

Using other factors

Other factors may be used. For example, you might want to rate frequency; however, you should consider each factor carefully in the context of the analysis. You should consider whether frequency would actually affect criticality of performance. In many jobs the critical activities are only rarely performed (such as an airline pilot having to crash land a plane).

Frequency of activity becomes important when considering retraining, because frequently performed activities do not require retraining if performance is at required standards. You might want to consider including some of the following factors in your analysis:

- actual time spent on the activity
- frequency of activity
- special training required
- relative time spent on the activity
- learning difficulty
- satisfaction gained from completing activity
- performer characteristics
- supervision required.

Having decided on your factors and agreed these with your analysis group, you can pilot test the activity inventory by asking several individuals to rate the activity statements and selected factors. You can then revise the activity inventory and eliminate possible and actual problem areas. The completed activity inventory can then be sent to a wider group for further rating.

Your sample for rating should be selected by one of the following procedures:

Random sampling: determine the size of your consultation population and select a random number across all contexts.

Stratified sampling: categorise the population into separate groups (ie, by length of employment/experience, location, etc), then randomly select a certain number from each category.

Once your consultation is complete, you should analyse the ratings and select those activities that require further analysis or training. These can be sorted according to priority, either by level of difficulty or by priority training need.

Interpreting the results of ratings
The following is a guide for interpreting your ratings:

1. *Very difficult and important.* These are the most critical. High importance means that analysis should continue and should consider job aids or job redesign as appropriate. High difficulty means that employees will probably require training in a simulated environment where the cost of failure is low.
2. *Very difficult but not important.* These are activities with a high level of difficulty so people will need training/retraining. As importance is low, however, the training can be done in the workplace. Continue the analysis to develop job aids.
3. *Moderately difficult and important.* These activities are quite critical. Analysis should result in job aids. The lower difficulty level suggests that training is needed, but in a safe, simulated environment.
4. *Moderately difficult but not important.* Formal training is not demanded for these activities, but it is still desirable. Low importance means that the training can be done safely in the workplace or on-the-job. Additional analysis may be needed to prepare training.
5. *Low difficulty but important.* These activities require little formal training because of low difficulty. High importance, however, demands that analysis continues to redesign the job or produce job aids so that the potential of serious consequences associated with possible error is reduced.
6. *Low difficulty and not important.* This means little training or job redesign is required of these activities, so analysis can stop here. On-the-job familiarisation is usually sufficient.
7. *Easy but important.* Training is almost never required for these activities, but the slight possibility of serious consequences of error exists, so analysis may continue to redesign jobs or prepare job aids.
8. *Easy and not important.* These activities do not require further analysis.

An example of a completed task inventory is shown in Figure 3.21.

ACTIVITY NUMBER	ACTIVITY	MEAN DIFFICULTY	MEAN IMPORTANCE	DECISION
1.1	Monitor System Operation	4.5	4.5	Continue analysis, job and equipment redesign, job aids and training
1.2	Stop System	1.5	4.6	Continue analysis, job aids, no further training
1.3				

Figure 3.21 *Example task inventory using risk assessment*

Advantages and disadvantages

Advantages

This technique allows the analyst to sort difficult and important tasks from easy and unimportant tasks, thus reducing the amount of analysis and training development time required and their associated costs.

Disadvantages

Since the response of various individuals is usually used to assess the important and difficulty of the tasks, uninformed opinion may dilute the accuracy of the results. Some important tasks may be eliminated from further analysis and eventual training. If this occurs, the costs associated with the resulting poor performance could increase.

Man-Machine Chart

When to use the man-machine chart

Use this technique when time is limited and when you need to analyse relationships between people, time and equipment. This is a technique specifically for use at skilled/craft level, and is useful for establishing standard work times.

How to use the man-machine chart

The analyst charts time to work activities. This requires the design of a man-machine time chart – the technique is shown in Figure 3.22.

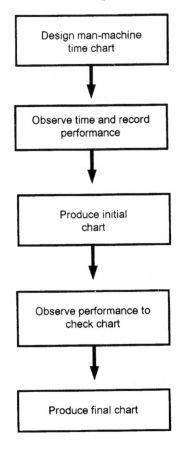

Figure 3.22 *Man-machine chart technique*

The chart you design should match the activity being analysed. You may have multiple columns. There should always be an individual time column for each person and 'machine' and a 'running time' for the observations. Examples of charts are illustrated in Figure 3.23.

Having observed and recorded time and performance (usually over several observations) the initial chart should be reviewed with the individuals concerned. Once agreed modifications are made, further observations should be undertaken to confirm the final chart.

Running Time	Description of Activity	Time
0 0.1 0.2 0.3	Task 1	0.5
	Task 2	0.6

Running Time	Operator	Time	Machine	Time
0 1	Activity 1	3	Idle	-
2 3	Activity 2	2	Start-up	0.5
4 5	Activity 3	2		2

Figure 3.23 *Examples of man-machine charts*

Advantages and disadvantages

Advantages
This is a relatively simple technique, useful in craft/skilled areas for establishing work times and therefore assisting with job redesign and/or training.

Disadvantages
This technique only works really well with sequential tasks and not with complex activities. The need to observe and review in the workplace can cause some disruption to normal work activity.

Flow Chart Technique

When to use the flow chart technique

Use this technique when you need to identify sequential activities. This is particularly useful if, for example, you want to conduct a functional analysis in an area in which you have limited experience. The technique helps provide you with a better understanding of the area to be analysed.

How to use the flow chart technique

The analyst produces a chart, through observation or discussion, which represents *only* those actions directly related to the 'flow' of performance. These actions are noted as active statements, each beginning with a verb.

It is usually best to aim for short statements. Each should be written in a rectangular box and connected by arrows which indicate 'flow' of activity. You might use index cards for each statement if you undertake the discussion with a group of role holders.

Contingencies need to be identified – these are written as questions: yes or no routes can then be identified and added to the chart. Alternative actions/behaviours which branch from each decision point should be identified. All branches must eventually lead back to the main 'flow' of statements, in the rectangular boxes. The symbols used in the chart are shown in Figure 3.24.

An example of the Flow Chart Technique, which relates to the competence-based assessment process, is given in Figure 3.25.

Advantages and disadvantages

Advantages
The Flow Chart Technique can be used on a one-to-one or group basis, requires full involvement, and can be operated at various levels of detail.

Disadvantages
Focus on process can lead to those involved concentrating on the incorrect perspective, eg if you want to develop functional statements (see Functional Analysis), then concentrating on process will confuse those involved.

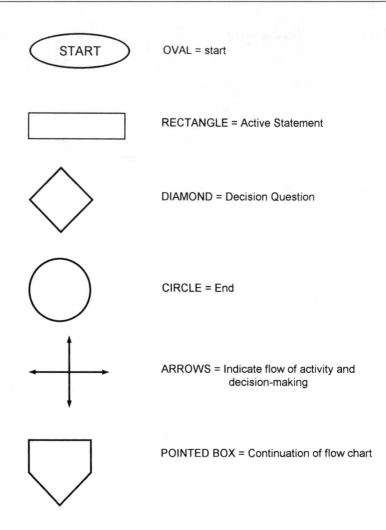

Figure 3.24 *Symbols of definition*

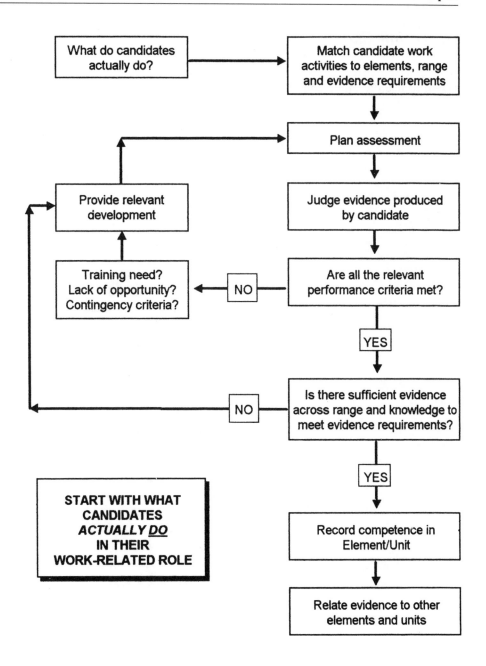

Figure 3.25 *Example flow chart*

Operation Chart

When to use the operation chart

Use this technique to record, categorise, monitor or plan improvements to actions and senses needed for skilled jobs. This is a useful technique for identifying 'performance criteria' (see Functional Analysis) or for preparing training programmes. Try video recording activities to reduce the time involved. The technique is illustrated in Figure 3.26.

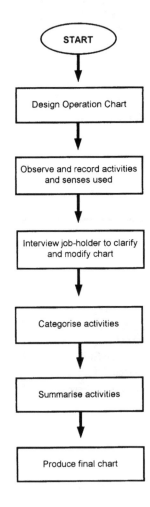

Figure 3.26 *Operation chart technique*

How to use the operation chart

Observe activities and record, in detail, activities and senses used.

Design your chart to suit the nature of the activities being analysed. The chart should have columns relating to right hand, left hand, type of activity, senses, time and any other critical factors. Do not go overboard on the design – stick with what is essential. An example chart is shown in Figure 3.27.

Activity Title:					
Left Hand	**Activity** **L**	**R**	**Right Hand**	**Senses**	**Comments**
TOTAL					

Figure 3.27 *Operation chart format*

Observe and record performance on your chart (in draft form). Immediately review your draft with the performer and categorise each activity. You might use symbols for this categorisation.

Summarise activities by adding categories for left hand or right hand, or sense used, for example.

Advantages and disadvantages

Advantages
The Operation Chart provides detailed analysis, including use of senses in work activities. This is very helpful when preparing training programmes or defining detailed measures of performance.

Disadvantages
This technique is best used for specific work activities which are sequential in nature. It can be time consuming.

Stimulus and Response

When to use the stimulus response chart

This technique provides a very detailed analysis of complex activities which involve numerous people, data inputs and decisions.

How to use the stimulus response chart

The analyst must, through observation, record the stimulus which leads to each detailed step of activity and the response that follows. Observation skills are therefore a key requirement.

Observe a job-holder undertaking the relevant work activity. List the basic sequence of actions performed (or video tape this to review later).

Review your list with the performer and chart the actual stimulus and response details.

On your chart indicate each stimulus (S) or initiating cue and the corresponding response (R). For example:

S ——————————————— **R**
Telephone rings   Answer telephone

Simple jobs will result in simple S–R as pairs. Complex jobns which involve decisions, selection from alternatives, etc will require more complex chains on the chart. For example:

S ——— R • S ——— R • S ——— R

This example outlines a chain of sequential stimulus-response pairs with no decision points.

Where decisions are involved (called 'discriminations' in this technique), these should be preceded by a vertical line. A discrimination is a decision that requires different responses to two or more related stimuli. A discrimination may not be observed during a single observation; identification will require observation over time and questioning. Your chart will develop along the lines of the following example in Figure 3.28.

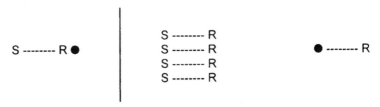

Figure 3.28 *Stimulus and response 1*

A 'generalisation' is a single response to multiple stimuli. You should indicate these by forked lines. Once again, questioning will be needed to elicit all relevant information. Your chart will look like Figure 3.29 when including a generalisation.

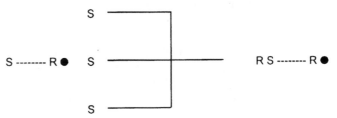

Figure 3.29 *Stimulus and response 2*

Multiple responses to a single stimulus are preceded by a vertical line and followed by another vertical line or dots, dependent upon the next stimulus in the sequence (Figure 3.30). Multiple responses may occur in any order but must be followed to a conclusion.

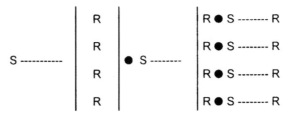

Figure 3.30 *Stimulus and response 3*

Completion of a S–R path is indicated by the symbol (END). Continuing a chain of S–R connections to a new page is indicated by a pointed box containing relevant references (Figure 3.31).

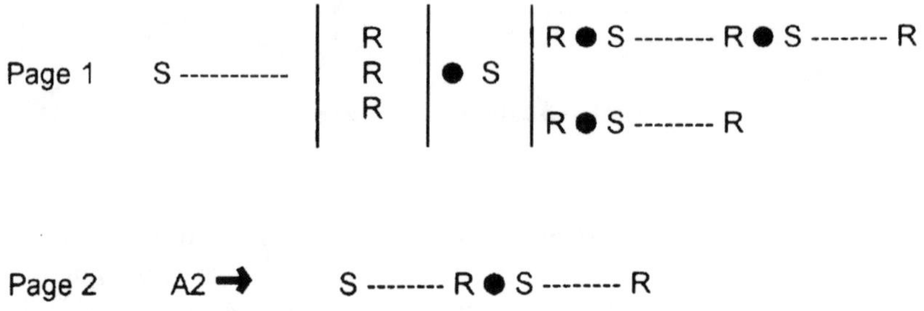

Page 1   S -----------   R   ● S -------- R ● S -------- R
                          R   ● S
                          R   R ● S -------- R

Page 2   A2 ➜   S -------- R ● S -------- R

Figure 3.31 *Stimulus and response 4*

A stimulus which starts a sequence is indicated by an asterisk. Responses should all be individually numbered in brackets. Numbering should be sequential until (END) is reached. Complex charts need to be put into data collection format (see Figure 3.32).

Advantages and disadvantages

Advantages
Useful for complex activities involving multiple actions and requiring complex decisions and selection from alternatives.

Disadvantages
This technique can be difficult to use at first.

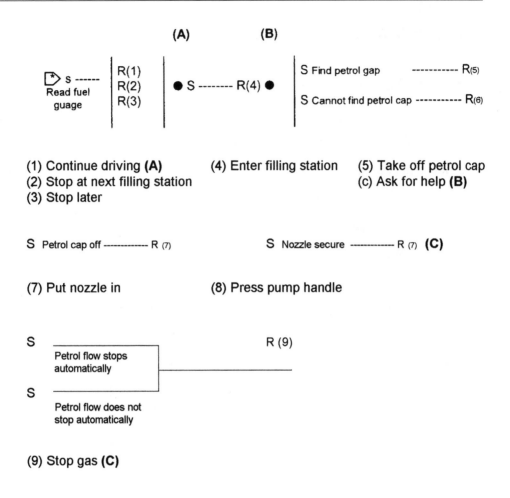

(A)   **(B)**

S ------ Read fuel guage

R(1)
R(2)
R(3)

● S -------- R(4) ●

S Find petrol gap   ----------- R(5)

S Cannot find petrol cap ----------- R(6)

(1) Continue driving **(A)**
(2) Stop at next filling station
(3) Stop later

(4) Enter filling station

(5) Take off petrol cap
(c) Ask for help **(B)**

S Petrol cap off ------------ R (7)

S Nozzle secure ------------ R (7) **(C)**

(7) Put nozzle in

(8) Press pump handle

S _____   Petrol flow stops automatically

R (9)

S _____   Petrol flow does not stop automatically

(9) Stop gas **(C)**

Figure 3.32 *Stimulus and response 5*

Decision Technique

When to use the decision technique

Use this technique to analyse non-sequential activities which involve making various decisions and selecting alternatives. This is a valuable technique for diagnostic purposes.

How to use the decision technique

This technique focuses the analyst's attention on the information needed to solve problems and produces a decision diagram. The technique is shown in Figure 3.33.

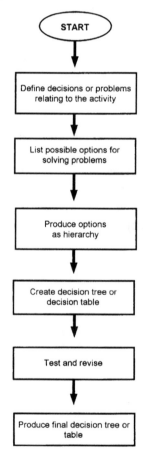

Figure 3.33 *Decision technique*

The first step is to define the decision to be analysed/solved. This will be a situation involving multiple stimuli or distinctions, and could be complex or simple activities. Ask job-holders questions such as:

- What could cause confusion in this activity?
- What options for action exist?
- What decisions must be made?

Write the answers to these questions as possible alternatives (or use alternatives generated by other techniques). You must then describe the differentiating characteristics of each alternative. For example, the following alternatives and characteristics relate to and distinguish between alternatives when deciding on travel arrangements from London to Manchester.

Drive: Control of journey, $2^1/_2$ hours journey time.

Fly: 45 minutes journey time plus time to/from airport.

Train: $1^1/_2$ hours journey time plus time to/from station.

Produce a hierarchy of options, basing this on discriminating characteristics which lead to the correct or most appropriate option. Each option has two parts: IF – THEN. For those familiar with computer programming, this will be recognisable as the basis of algorithms used to instruct computer applications (see also Flow Chart Technique).

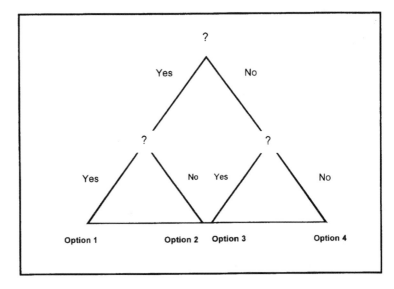

Figure 3.34 *Decision tree*

Some decisions will involve multiple criteria, for example:

If (alternative) and If (alternative) and If (alternative)
then (action).

This type of multiple criteria use is found in computer database software. Those of you who produce reports on databases will be familiar with a selection of multiple criteria in this way.

Charting is a means of describing options and there are various formats to use. These are normally called 'Decision tables' or 'Decision traces'. In the initial stages a 'Decision tree' is easier to use (see Figure 3.34). You might work with a group of performers to brainstorm 'if – then' statements and produce decision trees. Further work will then be needed to translate these into decisions charts/tables (see Figure 3.35).

If	Then
A	1
B	2

If	And If	Then
A	B C	1
B	C E	2

If	And If	And If	Then
A	B	F	1
	D	G	2
		J	3

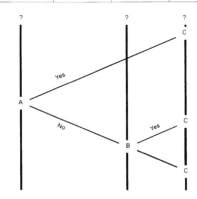

Figure 3.35 *Decision chart formats*

Advantages and disadvantages

Advantages
Useful for situations involving complex decisions. Describes activities conceptually and reduces complex information to a manageable format. Valuable job and training aids in final format.

Disadvantages
This technique does not include procedural information and the resulting charts can be misunderstood by those new to their use.

Critical Path Analysis

When to use critical path analysis

Use critical path analysis to analyse performance which has a definable beginning and end, and which involves a number of interrelated but distinct activities. It is helpful in functional or role analysis. Also use critical path analysis for designing or updating procedures and processes.

How to use critical path analysis

The basis of critical path analysis is the preparation of a network diagram in which each activity is represented by an arrow. The arrangement of arrows indicates the sequence of activities and their interdependency. Time estimates for each activity are added and the overall time is calculated.

First draw the logic of the activity on a 'network', basing this on the 'activity' and each 'event'. Draw from left to right (Figure 3.36 gives an example).

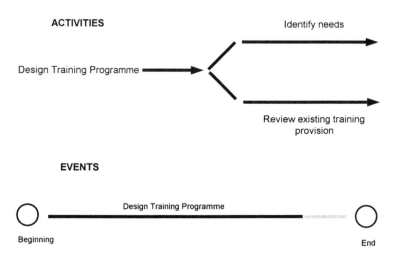

Figure 3.36 *Critical path analysis 1*

The beginning and end of *activities* are called events and symbolised by circles. Each point of achievement is also called an event and symbolised in the same way (Figures 3.37 and 3.38).

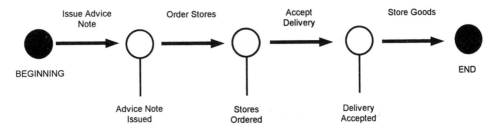

Figure 3.37 *Critical path analysis 2*

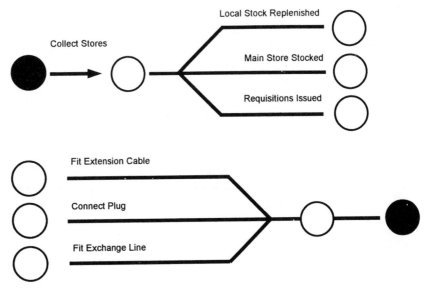

Figure 3.38 *Critical path analysis 3*

It is important to identify where events are *dependent* upon other events completion. Dependencies can be included in your network as shown in Figure 3.39. This indicates that A and B must be completed before C can start; B must be completed before D can start, but D is not dependent on completion of A.

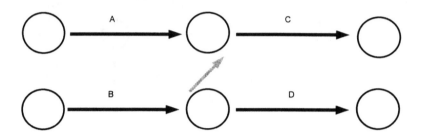

Figure 3.39 *Critical path analysis 4*

Each event is numbered sequentially (Figure 3.40). The sequence of event numbers in a network is not significant, simply convenient. The identify of each activity, however, must be unique. In the example shown in Figure 3.41, two different activities are labelled as 2, 3 (the parallel activities have common numbering). This should be corrected to look like Figure 3.42. In this revision, the logic of the activity remains correct, but each activity has a unique identify.

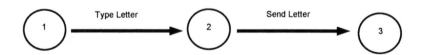

Figure 3.40 *Critical path analysis 5*

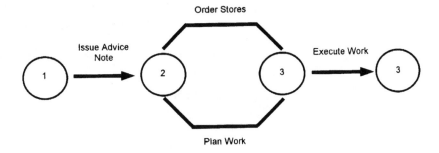

Figure 3.41 *Critical path analysis 6*

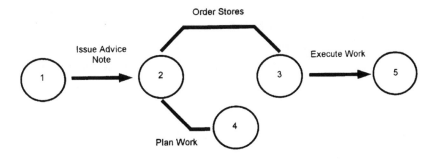

Activity 1, 2 - Issue Advice Note

Activity 2, 3 - Order Stores

Activity 2, 4 - Plan Work

Activity 3, 5 - Execute Work

Figure 3.42 *Critical path analysis 7*

To draw your network: Break down the function with role-holders and list the key activities. Note the sequence of activities and the constraints that apply, eg, interdependencies.

Select an activity and build up the network by asking the following questions:

- which activities must be completed before this activity can start?
- which activities may start at the same time as this activity?
- which activities may start as soon as this activity is completed?

If you wish to consider timing (or you are using this tool as a project management technique) you may then wish to schedule activities by allocating timing to each activity.

Advantages and disadvantages

Advantages
A useful technique in areas of complex activity. Lends itself to both task- and function-based analysis.

Disadvantages
Level of detail can be time consuming. Use of results will be confusing to the novice user.

3.3 Restructuring Components

3.3.1 Improving the Job/Role

Performance Probe

Behaviour Counting

Matrix Technique

Problem Analysis Technique

Repertory Grids

3.3.2 Learning the Job/Role

Critical Incident Analysis

Fault Tree Technique

Imagination Technique

Guided Training Aid

3.3.1 Improving the Job/Role

Performance Probe Technique

When to use the performance probe technique

Use this to assess resource, information, and motivation requirements of both role and role-holder in order to plan improvements.

How to use a performance probe technique

First, identify possible improvements and solutions to problems proposed by role-holders (see Figure 3.43) and categorise these. Second, describe the current role situation against each category (use previous analysis results to assist with this).

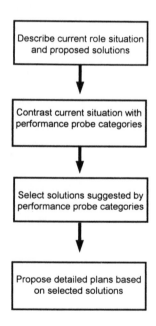

Figure 3.43 *Performance probe technique*

Next, select appropriate solutions for problems identified. Solutions should be ordered as follows:

(a)   Information solutions
(b)   Resource solutions
(c)   Incentive solutions
(d)   Training solutons
(e)   Personnel solutions
(f)   Motivation solutions.

This ordering is important as changes in earliest categories will influence later ones.

Finally, propose detailed plans for implementation. Your plan should clearly show the specific concerns and needs of the role.

1. INFORMATION PROBES	DESCRIBE CURRENT SITUATION
1. Work instructions are relevant, sufficient, accurate, user-friendly, accessible, up-to-date.	1. Clear work instructions not available
Solutions: Revise and produce work instructions	
PLAN BASED ON INFORMATION PROBES	
Working group, comprising one member for each context of this role to meet reguarly to produce work instructions.	

2. RESOURCE PROBES	DESCRIBE CURRENT SITUATION
Solutions:	
PLAN BASED ON INFORMATION PROBES	

Continue with other probe categories

Figure 3.44 *Example of performance probe job aid*

Advantages and disadvantages

Advantages

A quick way to assess needs using predefined categories to plan improvements.

Disadvantages

Often identifies real problems that management may currently be unwilling to address. Focuses attention of role-holders on problems more than on solutions.

Behaviour Counting Technique

When to use the behaviour counting technique

Use this technique to define differences between effective and ineffective work performance and to determine whether behaviours *actually* influence performance results.

How to use the behaviour counting technique

First, you will need to identify the behaviours which impact on and influence the role requirements. Work with managers and identified 'master performers' to agree observable behaviours relating to *inputs* to the role, to the process and to the outputs. Select the behaviours by asking the following questions:

- Can the behaviour be seen?
- Can the behaviour be measured?

If the answer to these two questions is 'No', you cannot use the behaviour for this type of analysis.

Next, identify role-holders who produce different outcomes. Include poor, average and excellent performers for your group. Make sure there is a real difference in results achieved across the group members. Important differences in results can be identified by measuring the PIP (Potential for Improving Performance). To do this, select one of the observable output measures you have agreed in step one and measure for both master performer and average performer (you might use regular reports for this information) then divide 'master' by 'average' output:

$$\frac{\text{Master Performer Output}}{\text{Average Performer Output}} = \text{PIP}$$

The resulting PIP measure tells you how much better the master performer's performance really is – hence 'Potential for Improving Performance'. A PIP of 1.0 means there is no difference between the master and average performer. A PIP of 4.0 would mean that the master performer is four times better.

Identify specific (critical) behaviours by observing role-holders at work. Count the occurrence of behaviours over a specific period or number of observations. Chart the behaviours per standard time for each performer. Use the vertical axis for the number of behaviours, and units of time on the horizontal axis.

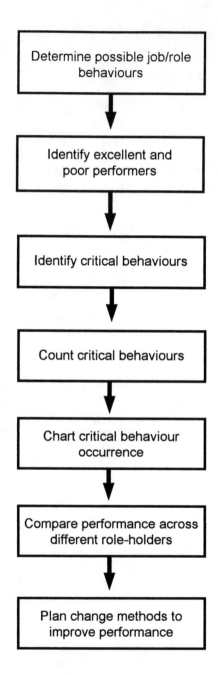

Figure 3.45 *Behaviour counting technique*

Compare charted behaviours of master, average and poor performers. Large differences indicate behaviours which contribute to differences in performance.

Plan the approach for improving behaviours – and thus performance.

Advantages and disadvantages

Advantages

This technique focuses on actual behaviours and attempts to produce measurable results. It is therefore useful for complex interpersonal skills-related roles.

Disadvantages

The focus on behaviour avoids looking at other possible faults and problems and will not help identify technical job-related skills deficiencies and training needs.

Matrix Technique

When to use the matrix technique

Use this technique to set a sequence of work activity or to establish ratings of the importance of work-related activities.

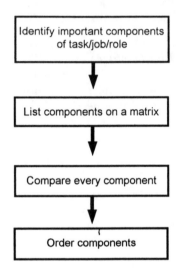

Figure 3.46 *Matrix technique*

How to use the matrix technique

Use the results of one or more of the previous techniques in this book to identify components of the task/job/role you are analysing. Any technique which identifies the *sequence* of activities will be appropriate (eg, Card Sort Technique).

Using graph paper, or a prepared matrix sheet, list all the components, or assign numbers and list these. The numbers should be written in serial order along a diagonal line of squares, starting at the top left corner and ending at the bottom right corner. An example is given in Figure 3.47.

1							Comments on Relationships
	2						
		3					
			4				
				5			
					6		
						7	

Figure 3.47 *Example matrix*

Compare *each* component with *every other* component to see if a relationship exists. Establish a 'relationship' by applying the following criteria:

- Is there a special type of relationship between the two components:
    - direct (one influences the other)?
    - symmetrical (both influence each other)?
    - indirect (both influenced by a third component)?
- Which is the most important component of the pair?

Note relationships on your matrix; see Figure 3.48, in which component number 2 is critical to virtually every component – it will therefore be essential that training in this component is provided for all role-holders.

1	×					
×	2	×	×		×	×
	×	3		×	×	
	×		4		×	
			×	5		
				×	6	
			×		×	7

Figure 3.48 *Completed matrix 1*

You may want to develop different matrices for different relationships you identify; see Figure 3.49, for example.

1.	Identify training need	1	X			X	X					
2.	Search menu of programmes		2	X	X	X						
3.	Consider options for delivery			3	X		X					
4.	Select appropriate programme				4	X						
5.	Arrange delivery					5						
6.	Evaluate outcome						6					

Figure 3.49 *Matrix 2 – direct relationships*

Once you have completed the comparison, order the components logically (eg, most important to least important, close relationship to indirect relationship).

Advantages and disadvantages

Advantages
Relationships and importance of task can easily be identified with this technique. It is particularly helpful for identifying critical components which should be prioritised for training.

Disadvantages
This can be a time consuming technique and can be confusing to the novice – which in turn would lead to subjective results.

Problem Analysis Technique

When to use the problem analysis technique

Use this technique to identify underlying reasons for faulty or incorrect performance.

How to use the problem analysis technique

Observe performance by a number of role-holders over a period of time to identify errors which occur. Label each error/problem – use a name which specifies the correct performance and what is wrong with current performance.

Describe each problem – what and where it occurs, when and how often it occurs, and its effects.

List any changes which preceded the problem, eg, change in personnel, equipment, etc.

List all distinctive features of the problem area.

Identify major influences on incorrect performance and identify the most probable causes of incorrect performance.

Identify 'evidence' which can be collected to support your judgements about probable causes and analyse the evidence.

Select the most probable cause(s) based on the evidence reviewed. Propose a plan for solving the problem.

Advantages and disadvantages

Advantages

This is a useful technique for solving problems in performance and for generating data which can contribute to training needs analysis/ training design.

Disadvantages

This technique is not intended as a tool for identifying or proposing correct performance or for redesign of jobs/roles. It should be presented positively, as the focus on problems/errors can be demotivating for role-holders.

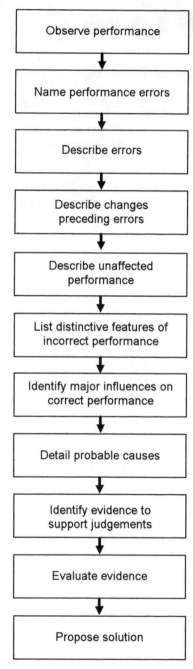

Figure 3.50 *Problem analysis technique*

Repertory Grids

When to use repertory grids

Use this technique when you want to develop behavioural competencies or when conducting analysis which needs data from individual perceptions of work and roles. You might use the results of analysis to help with selection, training design, evaluation, workbased assessment.

How to use repertory grids

A repertory grid is a method of obtaining an individual's personal 'constructs' and subjecting them to analysis to produce an objective map. Using the grid with groups of role-holders can provide a consensus of key behaviours and expectations of performance.

There are five stages to the repertory grid process. This can be quite complex, but is often simplified to meet specific needs:

1. Elicit the elements
2. Elicit the constructs
3. Prepare the grid
4. Analyse the grid.

1. Eliciting the elements

The first stage in the use of personal constructs is to elicit the 'objects' or, technically, the elements of a person's thoughts. Eliciting the elements is extremely important because it lays the ground work for all the other stages. An error in this first stage can invalidate all subsequent work and conclusions. Because the elicitation of the elements is apparently simple, little thought has been given to the process and very few guidelines are available.

Typically, elicitation of the elements consists of asking the subject to list all the people that he or she considers important in a certain domain. For example, 'Please write down all the people who you think have an important effect on the way you carry out your job as a supervisor.'

There are some obvious points of difficulty:

- The subject must be able to understand what is required, so use short words and short technical terms or acronyms. Be sensitive to subtle but important differences in the shades of meaning. For example, the subject's definition of his or her role may contain a rather unexpected constellation of activities.

- How important is important? Quite subtle cues can influence the subject. If a subject is given a form with 20 spaces on it, he or she will probably list more people as being important than on a form with only 16 spaces on it.
- The use of examples may make your requirements clearer to the subject, but may have a biasing effect. If you decide to use an example, it is probably best to choose one that is remote from the aim of the study even though this runs the risk of the subject feeling that your example is ridiculous.

In general, it is probably better to err on the generous side, and ask for elements from a slightly wider scope than the investigation seems to require. In any event, it is necessary to always bear in mind that the 'universe' from which the elements were drawn may constrain the conclusions which can be made.

2. Eliciting the constructs

The usual method of eliciting the constructs involves first writing each element down on a separate card. Three stages then follow for each of the constructs elicited:

- shuffle the cards and present three chosen at random to the subject and ask him or her to *indicate the element* which is *the odd one out*
- ask the subject to say *why* the element he has chosen is the odd one out; this produces the construct
- *check the meaning of the construct:* some are ambiguous. If I describe someone as 'Conservative', it could be that they vote Tory, or it could be merely someone that prefers established values, or both. Not all ambiguities are as obvious. Two techniques for checking the meaning are:
  - ask the subject for any words that mean the same (ie, a simile) as the construct he or she has just given;
  - ask the subject for concrete benchmarks for the construct eg, 'Imagine a person who is very XXX. How would this show in their behaviour? Imagine a person who has no XXX at all. How would this show?'

Besides checking the meaning, this additional information makes it easier to check the range of convenience (basically, the scope of your analysis) and to interpret the results.

This cycle will be repeated with another random triad of elements.

When to terminate elicitation of constructs There is no foolproof indication that shows that all the important constructs have been elicited. In principle it can take a very long time. There are 720 possible random triads, from just ten elements. In practice the elicitation of constructs is terminated either:

- when the same construct is repeatedly elicited, or

- when the rapport between subject and tester is likely to be strained. In actual fact, most of the details of a construct system can be obtained from eight to ten constructs.

3. Preparing and administering the grid

Once the list of elements and constructs has been elicited, the next stage is to get the respondent to fill in the grid. Until recently grids have been administered individually; however, there is a growing trend towards the administration of 'supplied' grids to groups of subjects as, for example, in the case of management training evaluation. This will be the case that will be outlined since it has some special problems and covers the procedure that should be adopted for individual grid completion.

Preparation of the grid If we assume that we have already elicited the elements and constructs, and are satisfied that these are the ones that are relevant to the group we wish to look at and cover any points that we may have certain hypotheses about, we must then prepare a grid for the group to fill in.

The first step is to design a grid form (an example is provided in Figure 3.51). It is advisable to work towards the standardised form if at all possible; the benefit of doing so is that not only does it save a considerable amount of time during the administration session itself, but it also helps in the later handling stages and often highlights the need for additional refinements to suit your particular system.

The second step is to fill in the actual names of the elements and constructs in spaces available on the form. The elements are filled in across the top of the grid, while the constructs are written down the side of the grid. There is no theoretical reason why this should be the case, but there is the important practical consideration that this is the form the data must be presented in for the subsequent computer analysis.

Setting the scene How the grid session is introduced is very important. If you are using a grid that is actually in the 'grid' or matrix form, as in our example, then you are presenting something that the subjects are

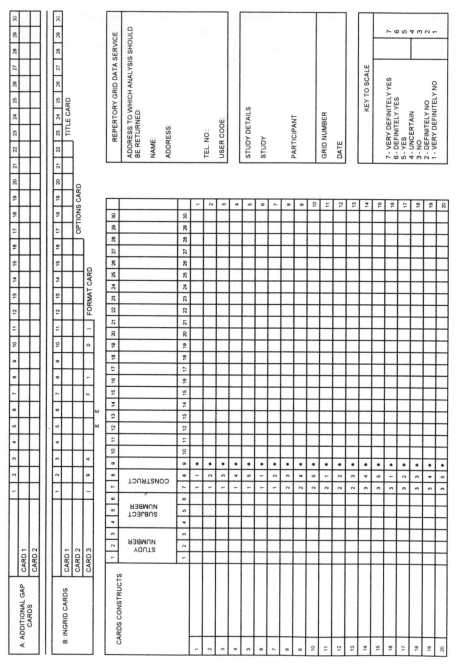

Figure 3.51 *An example of a repertory grid form*

not likely to have met before, unlike standard questionnaire scales. The best approach is to use a matter-of-fact attitude avoiding the use of jargon phrases such as 'repertory grids', 'constructs,' etc. At best, the use of these terms may delay the proceedings, while the subjects learn the new terms; often it may frighten or confuse them.

So, one way of introducing the grid in a training situation is to say something like the following:

> 'We are now going to ask you to complete a questionnaire. Its *purpose* is to help us to find out the views of managers about various aspects of the work situation.

> 'Your participation in this questionnaire exercise is entirely voluntary but we hope you will take part since it is obviously very important to take notice of what our managers think.

> 'We can assure you that any information you give us will be kept strictly confidential. No one outside of our research division will have access to any of the information you give us, so none of your colleagues or bosses will know what you say to us. We are only concerned with the views of groups of people and so no one will be able to be identified in any subsequent reports we produce.

> 'Since it is your opionions and attitudes we are interested in, there are *no right or wrong answers*. We hope, therefore, you will feel that this is an opportunity to express your views openly and frankly.'

Presenting the grid   Having set the scene and assured yourself that everyone is happy with what they are being asked to do, the next stage is to present the actual grid. How you present it to a large extent determines how long it will take to complete it. Any time spent here can avoid the quite familiar effects of 'shell-shock' when subjects are presented with something which is complicated and unfamiliar to them. Experience has shown us that, when badly presented, grids of about 15 x 15 can take between one and one and a half hours to complete, while following certain basic rules can reduce this to about 30 minutes. I therefore suggest that, when possible, these stages are followed:

1. Use an overhead projector and present a slide showing a list of elements only. This helps to ensure that the subjects are familiar with the terminology used on the grids, and don't rush into grid marking, rating elements on what they think they've read rather than on what is written. Each element should be read out in full so as to make clear any abbreviations used.

2. Step 1 should be repeated for all the constructs.

3. Then explain that the elements and constructs are combined on a grid and that each construct is used to describe each element. Present a grid containing both the elements and constructs and explain that each element is to be rated on each construct. This is the stage at which 'shock' is most likely to occur. One of our course tutors commented on this by saying, 'Several course members recoiled a little; the grid must have seemed a formidable thing at first sight'. It is recommended that the slide is left on for a few minutes while the elements and constructs are read out again, and the instructions for completing the grid are also repeated.

4. Once these explanations have been given, the grid forms should be handed out. The subjects should then be asked to rate the first element on the first construct with the rider that if they can think of actual people then so much the better. When they have filled in their response they should be asked to work across the first row rating all the elements on that first construct. A piece of coloured card is useful to help them to follow the row across without getting lost (especially important for large grids). If they are happy with the procedure they are then asked to complete the rest of the grid working across one row at a time, making sure that every square has a number it.

Indeed, the need for careful presentation to avoid spurious markings is felt to be so important that it has been suggested that there ought to be at least one 'dummy' construct at the beginning of the grid to ensure familiarisation prior to using the relevant constructs.

Additionally, it will be realised that it may well matter which way the grid is filled in. Filling in a column first (ie, rating one element on all constructs) effectively produces a 'profile' rating; while filling in a row first (rating all elements on one construct) may produce 'relative' markings which highlight the differences between elements.

You might modify this approach in many ways, perhaps by providing a predesigned form for individuals to use.

The following prompt sheet (Figure 3.52) and example grid (Figure 3.53) may give you some ideas.

Possible descriptors

works with the team	prefers to work alone
controls all activity	delegates activities appropriately
receptive to feedback	difficulty accepting feedback
customer-focused	sells products and services
keeps everyone informed	forgets others' need to know
friendly	unfriendly
open and honest	keeps people in the dark
proactive	reactive
results-orientated	works day-to-day
enthusiastic	gets the job done eventually
seeks help when needed	tries to solve problems alone
task-focused	solution-focused
joins in to meet pressured demands	lets others deal with pressure
welcomes changes	avoids change at all costs
open to new ideas	stays with the tried and trusted
tidy and organised	untidy and loses things
short-term view	long-term view
consistent	unpredictable
aims for complete task	aims for quality
explores potential and possibilities	not confident in new areas
achieves in defined area	constantly seeks new challenges
leads by example	has double standards
jumps in with both feet	considers all options before acting
seeks responsibility	avoids responsibility
encourages others' ideas	directs others

Figure 3.52 *Prompt sheet*

FUNCTION				
INITIALS OF THREE PEOPLE				
What do the pair have in common?				What makes the odd one out different?

Figure 3.53 *An example of a grid*

4. Analysing the results
If you use the full scale repertory grid technique you will plot individual responses on a 'cognitive map'; an example is given in Figure 3.54. This map shows dimensions in an individual's construct system.

If you use the simpler example, you will analyse the group results to find consensus on key behaviours/attributes. These will form the basis of your competencies.

Advantages and disadvantages

Advantages
This is a detailed approach which can be modified to suit many contexts. It can be used with individuals or groups.

Disadvantages
Can be complex to use and requires statistical analysis skills if the full model is implemented.

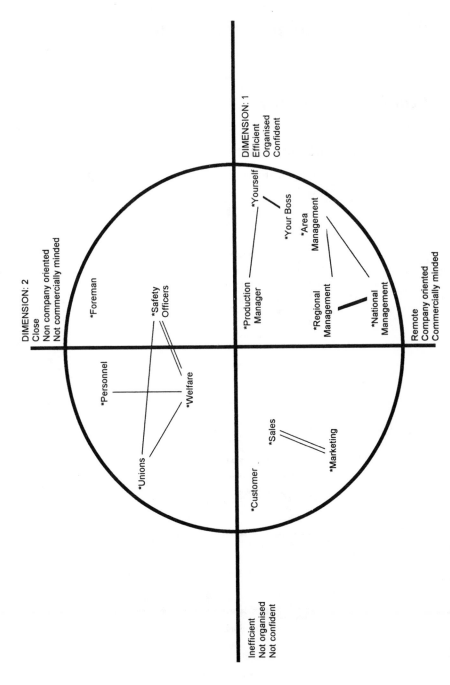

Figure 3.54 *Cognitive map*

3.3.2   Learning the Job/Role

Critical Incident Analysis

When to use critical incident analysis

Use this technique to identify excellent and poor performance and the underlying causes.

Name .... Date ....

Key function	

Good Incident Worksheet

Circumstances of incident	
What was done	
Outcome	
What enabled good performance	
What hard evidence demonstrated this good performance	

Poor Incident Worksheet

Circumstances of incident	
What was done	
Outcome	
What influenced ineffective performance	

Figure 3.55 *Critical incident worksheet*

How to use critical incident analysis

This technique can be used with individuals, pairs or groups. Provide each person/pair/group with copies of the critical incident analysis worksheet (see Figure 3.55).

Ask participants to note each of the components listed at the top of one sheet – one per sheet.

Ask participants to complete the details on the sheet, illustrating one example of good/excellent performance and one of poor/ineffective performance.

Analyse the results of analysis using one of the earlier techniques in this book (eg, Functional Analysis, Card Sort). Collate the responses to identify key aspects/enablers of performance as well as critical aspects to be avoided.

Advantages and disadvantages

Advantages
This is a simple and quick approach to identify key underlying behaviours and enablers.

Disadvantages
May present some difficulties if there are any 'punitive' aspects of analysis in respect of ineffective performance examples.

Fault Tree Technique

When to use the fault tree technique

Use this technique to identify potential causes of failure or ineffective performance. Useful for job redesign.

How to use the fault tree technique

Work with master performers to identify possible reasons for failure or ineffective performance. Produce a fault tree diagram.

Start by identifying a critical event/action which could cause failure and generate ideas on possible causes. Determine the relationship between the critical event and possible causes of failure and explore the 'problem paths'. Recommend changes based on your analysis.

A fault tree diagram uses specific symbols shown in Figure 3.56. An example of the symbols in use in a fault tree is given in Figure 3.57.

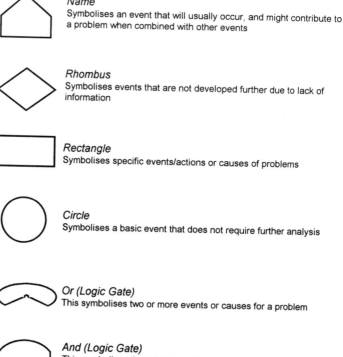

Name
Symbolises an event that will usually occur, and might contribute to a problem when combined with other events

Rhombus
Symbolises events that are not developed further due to lack of information

Rectangle
Symbolises specific events/actions or causes of problems

Circle
Symbolises a basic event that does not require further analysis

Or (Logic Gate)
This symbolises two or more events or causes for a problem

And (Logic Gate)
This symbolises the existence of two or more events/causes which must co-exist to influence a larger problem

Figure 3.56 *Fault tree symbols*

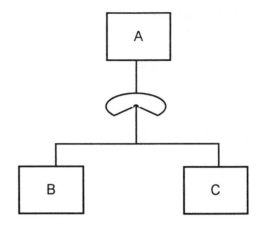

Event A will happen if either Event B or Event C occurs

Figure 3.57 *Example of a fault tree*

Advantages and disadvantages

Advantages
As a graphic tool it is a useful way to involve a wide range of people and to explore the interrelationships of role components.

Disadvantages
Unfamiliarity with the symbols can lead to confusion.

Imagination Technique

When to use the imagination technique

Use this technique to plan ahead and focus on the 'ideal' performance in a role or when an innovative approach to performance is needed.

How to use the imagination technique

Create a function/task list using one of the earlier techniques in this book. Run a workshop with a group of role-holders. Choose an environment that is relaxing and encourages creative working.

Ask participants to relax and think about what a specific function/task in their role would be like in an 'ideal' world. Ask them to imagine:

- who would do what
- when
- how
- where
- what is seen, heard.

Ensure that no criticism is made when you ask participants to describe their ideal role context. Encourage creativity and do not censor ideas. However, avoid a discussion of problems – focus on solutions.

Record the outcomes in a format such as the example shown in Figure 3.58.

Advantages and disadvantages

Advantages

This technique encourages innovation and creativity and does not focus on problems. A good technique for job redesign.

Disadvantages

Some people may feel uncomfortable in this type of situation, particularly if there is a lack of trust or experience of the group.

Function/Task	

Ideal Method	Current Method

Differences	Advantages	Disadvantages

Figure 3.58 *Imagination chart*

Guided Training Aid Technique

When to use the guided training aid technique

Use this technique to collate results of analysis and prepare a job aid to help with training.

How to use the guided training aid technique

Get training ready
Unveil the task
Illustrate the task
Direct practice
Explore questions
Document the training.

Use the tasks identified from the application of techniques outlined earlier in this book.

Take each task in turn and record it at the top of a training card. List items required to perform the task. List reasons for performing the task and benefits of completing it competently. Note all steps required to complete the task.

List questions about problem areas – 'What if...'. Provide assessment criteria relating to the quality of successful outcome of performance. Provide directions for the trainer.

An example of a Guided Training Aid is shown in Figure 3.59 (page 111).

Advantages and disadvantages

Advantages
This technique provides a simple training/memory aid. It also provides a format for the results of your analysis techniques which can be used by trainers and workplace assessors.

Disadvantages
This can be used inappropriately. Its purpose is as an aid to improve performance by identifying specific aspects for improvement.

Record Contact with Sales Prospect

Benefits

	Get training ready
Provides reference for discussion or telephone contact. Records agreement and action agreed. Acts as a reminder. Increases efficiency.	Unveil task steps
	Illustrate tasks
	Direct practice
	Explore questions
	Document training

Tools, Equipment, Materials

Contact record sheet - paper-based or computerised

Steps   **Pictures/Script**

Steps	Pictures/Script
1. Before a meeting, or after a telephone call, enter contact details (date, name, location, time) on contact record	**Contact Record** Name .... Company .... Telephone .... Fax ....
2. Record date of contact	
3. Record details of contact	**Contact Details**
4. Record next action	Date Details Action
5. Follow up and implement	

Discussion Questions   **Trainer Recommendation**

Discussion Questions	Trainer Recommendation
What if I try to contact a prospect and they are not available? What if I cannot follow up?	

Employee Performance   **Training Needed**

Employee Performance	Training Needed
Excellent Competent Training needs identified	

Figure 3.59 *Record of contact with sales prospect – an example of a guided training aid*

Quick Reference Chart

When your need is...	Try...
To develop function-based competences, either outcome- or behaviour-based	Functional Analysis Critical Incident
To contrast the role against standardised work classifications to check full coverage	Job Function Technique Fault Tree Technique
To assess the need for additional analysis	Risk Assessment Technique
To prepare job aids to help improve performance	Guided Training Aid Technique
To break down a wide variety of role activities and related equipment	Walk and Talk Technique
To produce a basic level task breakdown	Task Matrix Technique
To produce a detailed task breakdown	List Expansion Technique
To produce a role analysis when no job descriptions exist and master performers are the main source of information	Interview Note Technique Functional Analysis
To analyse a role or job which has many interrelated activities (eg, managerial)	Daily Log Technique Job Function Technique Functional Analysis
To analyse the effects of behaviour on performance	Behaviour Counting Technique
To categorise performance and identify potential improvements	Critical Path Analysis Critical Incident Technique
To identify specific performance problems	Problem Analysis Technique Performance Probe Technique
To anticipate potential areas of problem	Fault Tree Technique
To innovate in respect of job methods	Imagination Technique
To gain consensus on the sequence of work activities	Matrix Technique Process Chart Technique
To produce a basic description of sequential tasks	Basic Task Description Technique
To analyse a basic description of multiple decisions, inputs or people	Stimulus/Response Technique
To analyse the sequence of activities, key decision points and alternative action points	Flow Chart Technique
To analyse activities which are non-sequential and involve concept-based thinking and decision making	Decision Technique
To analyse time and man-machine interfaces	Man-Machine Time Chart
To analyse the interrelationship of activities and behaviour inputs	Repertory Grid

References and Further Reading

Annerman, H L and Pratzner, F L (1977) *Performance Content for Job Training*, 5 Vols. Columbus, OH: Center for Vocational Education, Ohio State University.

Annett, J and Duncan, K D (1968) Task Analysis: A Critique, in Barnes, J and Robinson, N (eds), *New Media and Methods in Industrial Training*, London: British Broadcasting Corporation.

Carlisle, K E (1981) Towards a Methodology for Assessing Consistency Between Multiple Network Matrix Task Analyses of the Same Task, unpublished Doctoral Dissertation, Indiana University.

Carlisle, K E (1982) The Learning Strategy Technique of Task Analysis, *NPSI Journal*, 1982, **21**, No. 10, 9–11 and 41.

Davies, I K (1973) *Competency Based Learning*, New York: McGraw-Hill.

D'Costa, A. G and Watson, J E (1983) A Critical-Incident Technique for Developing Criterion-Referenced Tests. *Educational Technology*, **23**, 7, 13–16.

Deden-Parker, A (1980) Needs Assessment in Depth: Professional Training at Wells Fargo Bank, *Journal of Instructional Development*, **1**, 1, 3–9.

Department for Education and Employment (DfEE) and Training Agency (1991) *Guidance on the Development of National Standards and NVQs*, Technical Advisory Group, London: DfEE.

Duncan, K (1972) Strategies for Analysis of a Task, in Hartley, J (ed.) *Strategies for Programmed Instruction: An Educational Technology*. London: Butterworths.

Fine, S A (1974) Functional Job Analysis: An Approach to a Technology for Manpower Planning, *Personnel Journal*, 1974, November, 813–18.

Fine, S A and Wiley, W W (1971) *An Introduction to Functional Job Analysis*, Kalamazoo, MI: W E Upjohn Institute for Employment Research.

Fleishman, E A (1978) Relating Individual Differences to the Dimensions of Human Tasks, *Ergonomics*, **21**, 12, 1007–1019.

Gagné, R M (1974) Task Analysis: Its Relation to Content Analysis, *Educational Psychologist*, 1974, **2**, 1, 11–18.

Gilbert, T F (1978) Measuring Potential for Performance Improvement, *Training/HRD*, December.

Hannum, W H (1974) Toward a Framework for Task Analysis, *Educational Technology*, **14**, 2, 57–58.

Harmon, P H (1983) Task Analysis: A Top-Down Approach, *Performance and Instruction Journal*, May, 14–19.

Hemphill, J K (1959) Job Descriptions for Executives, *Harvard Business Review*, **37**, 55–67.

Hoffman, C K and Medsker, K L (1983) Instructional Analysis: The Missing Link Between Task Analysis and Objectives, *Journal of Instructional Development*, **6**, 4, 17–24.

Kennedy, P, Esque, T and Novak, J (1983) A Functional Analysis of Task Analysis Procedures for Instructional Design, *Journal of Instructional Development*, **6**, 4, 10–16.

King Taylor, L (1973) *Not for Bread Alone: An Appreciation of Job Enrichment*, London: Business Books.

McCormick, E J (1979) *Job Analysis: Methods and Applications*, New York: AMACOM.

McCormick, E J, Jeanneret, P R and Mecham, R C (1972) A Study of Job Characteristics and Job Dimensions as Based on the Position Analysis Questionnaire (PAQ), *Journal of Applied Psychology*, **56**, 347–368.

McDermott, F M (1982) Try Brainstorming: A Quick Route to Job Analysis, *Training/HRD*, **19**, 3, 39–40.

Mallory, W J (1982) A Task-Analytic Approach to Specifying Technical Training Needs, *Training and Development Journal*, September, 66–73.

Markowitz, J (1981) Four Methods of Job Analysis, *Training and Development Journal*, September, 112–118.

Melching, W H and Borcher, S D (1973) *Procedures for Constructing and Using Task Inventories*, Center for Vocational and Technical Education, Research and Development Series No. 91. Columbus, Ohio: Ohio State University.

Murray-Hicks, M (1981) Analysis Techniques for Management Skills, *NPSI Journal*, May, 16–20.

Niebel, B W (1962) *Motion and Time Study*, Homewood, IL: Richard D Irwin.

Paul, W J and Robertson, K B (1970) *Job Enrichment and Employee Motivation*, Epping, UK: Gower Press.

Peterson, R O and Duffany, B H (1976) Job Enrichment and Redesign, in Craig, R L (ed.) *Training and Development Handbook*, New York: McGraw-Hill, 15.1–15.15.

Reason, J (1977) Skill and Error in Everyday Life, in Howe, J J A (ed.) *Adult Learning: Psychology Research and Applications*, New York: John Wiley and Sons.

Resnick, L B, Wang, M C and Kaplan, J (1973) Task Analysis in Curriculum Design: A Hierarchically Sequenced Introductory Mathematics Curriculum, *Journal of Applied Behaviour Analysis*, **6**, 4, 679–710.

Robinson, A D (1984) What You See Is What You Get, *Training and Development Journal*, May, 34–39.

Shepard, A (1976) An Improved Tabular Format for Task Analysis, *Journal of Occupational Psychology*, **49**, 93–104.

Siegler, R S (1980) Recent Trends in the Study of Cognitive Development: Variations on a Task Analytic Time, *Human Development*, **23**, 4, 278–285.

Solomon, G and Bouloutian, A (1982) Build a Performance System – Not a Training System, *Training and Development Journal*, September, 32–34.

Spitzer, D (1980) Try Fault Tree Analysis, a Step-By-Step Way to Improve Organisational Development, *Training/HRD*, February, 58–69.

Stainer, F W (1967) Training for Fault Diagnosis, *Proceedings of the Institute of Electrical Engineers*, 114.

Stephens, K G (1972) A Fault Tree Approach to Analysis of Educational Systems as Demonstrated in Vocational Education, unpublished Doctoral Dissertation, University of Washington.

Stone, C H and Yoder, D (1970) *Job Analysis 1970*, Long Beach, CA: California State College.

Task Analysis: Training's Enduring Workhorse, *Training/HRD*, (1982) February, 80–83.

Terrel, W R (1983) Algorithmic Processes for Increasing Design Efficiency, *Journal for Instructional Development*, **6**, 2, 33–41.

Tiemann, P and Markle, S (1978) *Analysing Instructional Content: A Guide to Instruction and Evaluation*, Champaign, IL: Stipes Publishing.

US Department of Labor (1972) *Handbook for Analysing Jobs*, Manpower Administration, Washington, DC: US Government Printing Office.

US Department of Labor (1973), *Task Analysis Inventories*, Manpower Administration. Washington DC: US Government Printing Office.

Utt, C T (1982) Flow-Process Charts; How They Help Determine Employee Training Needs, *Training/HRD*, January, 80–81.

Van Gundy, A B (1981) *Techniques of Structured Problem Solving*, New York: Van Nostrand-Reinhold.

Wilson, A and Goodman, R L (1984) Task-Unit Scheduling for Improved Service and Productivity, *The Cornell HRA Quarterly*, August, 78–83.

Yaney, J P (1974) A Critical Review of the Instructional Technology Mechanism of Task Analysis, *Improving Human Performance: A Research Quarterly*, **3**, 2, 64–70.

Zemke, R (1974) The Critical Incident Method of Analysis, *Training/HRD*, April.

Zemke, R (1976) Behavioural Observations: Why the 'Count and Chart' Approach to Task Analysis Pays Off, *Training/HRD*, September, 90–93.

Zemke, R and Kramlinger, T (1982) *Figuring Things Out: A Trainer's Guide to Needs and Task Analysis*, Reading, MA: Addison-Wesley.

Zerga, J (1943) Job Analysis: A Resume and Bibliography, *Journal of Applied Psychology*, **27**, 249–267.